böhlau

Aleksandra Skrzypietz (ed.)

Queens within Networks of Family and Court Connections

Böhlau Verlag Wien Köln

UNIVERSITY OF SILESIA
IN KATOWICE

The publication was financially supported by the University of Silesia in Katowice.

Bibliographic information published by the Deutsche Nationalbibliothek:
The Deutsche Nationalbibliothek lists this publication in the Deutsche Nationalbibliografie; detailed bibliographic data available online: https://dnb.de.

Cover design: Michael Haderer, Wien
Scientific review: Marian Chachaj (Maria Curie-Sklodowska University) and
Bogdan Rok (University of Wrocław)
Proofreading: Uli Nickel, Münster
Typesetting: le-tex publishing services, Leipzig

Printed and bound: Hubert & Co. BuchPartner, Göttingen
Printed in the EU

Vandenhoeck & Ruprecht Verlage | www.vandenhoeck-ruprecht-verlage.com
ISBN 978-3-412-52390-9

Contents

Acknowledgements

I would like to thank everyone involved in the making of this volume sincerely. First and foremost, I would like to thank all the authors who were willing to share their research on queens and networks of connections, in which they found themselves at their courts and in family arrangements.

This publication would not have been possible without the help and support of the Faculty of Humanities Dean from the University of Silesia, Associate Professor Adam Dziadek, who allocated funds to have this volume translated and printed. Thanks are also due to Assistant Professor Renata Dampc-Jarosz, for all the help she offered.

Pursuant to the best tradition of Polish academic studies, all the articles have been reviewed. This task was carried out by the specialists in the Early Modern Period, Associate Professor Marian Chachaj and Associate Professor Bogdan Rok, who shared their knowledge and experience with us. I wish to thank them for their valuable remarks and their commitment to this project.

Thanks are also due to the translator of these articles, Dr Anna Miączewska.

Aleksandra Skrzypietz

Introduction

A figure of a queen, a monarch's wife, enjoys an unfailing interest from historians. Many of these women were to win influence and power using various tools often not attached to their position. Therefore, it seems interesting and important to trace the steps that could lead them to power or give them an opportunity to achieve the goals they set for themselves. It is often not enough to show the way in which queen consort influenced her surroundings, it is also significant to determine people whom she used for that purpose and through whom she tried to reach for influence and power.[1] On the other hand, each queen was subjected to the impact of her circles; relatives, courtiers, and many other people tried to reach the ruler through the queen, and his spouse was to open up to them the possibility of influencing him. Thus, scholars try to present the queens' role in the royal court environment, they seek for manifestations of their probable – and sometimes almost imperceptible – influence on their husbands and their actions, and they try to determine which queens created their own networks of connections and pressures in order to gain control, and which gave in to the pressure of their surroundings and played a role of intermediaries in exercising power or successfully defended themselves from those influences and refused to intercede on behalf of somebody else.

Traditional roles of royal consorts came down to building political alliances between families and states, from which they originated and those they entered through marriage. The dowry of a given candidate, which – as expected – was to contribute to the husband's treasury, was often an element not deprived of its relevance in finalising the royal marriage. Crumbling political alliances and unpaid dowries could be the cause of tensions and problems of queens, who disappointed their husbands, their families and advisers, completely regardless of their wills, wishes, and possibilities. The major aim of every monarchical relationship was the birth of a male heir, although daughters – as long as not too numerous – could also become a political asset. Wives who failed to comply with these tasks – did not provide political support, did not bring in the promised dowry or did not give birth to an heir – were doomed to an uncertain future and their position was

1 Some of the materials used in this book have been prepared as part of the 2018/29/B/HS3/00907 project: Polish Courtier at the Royal Courts of the Jagiellons and Elective Kings: Rank, Value System, Role Model (Dworzanin polski na dworze Jagiellonów i królów elekcyjnych. Pozycja, system wartości, wzorzec osobowy), financed by the National Science Centre.

inevitably weakened. Women who experienced this became victims of unfavourable and sometimes tragic circumstances.

The queen was responsible for representation duties. Participating in public and court ceremonies by her husband's side, or on her own should the situation require it, in charity and devotional functions, particularly fulfilling religious duties sometimes even quite demonstratively, was part of the royal consort's everyday life. Appropriate creation of an image of a wife and mother, placing emphasis on the loyalty towards her husband and Church, the splendour of garments and jewels presenting the magnificence and – not always realistic – possibilities of the royal consort, were the everyday life elements and tasks facing the queens.[2] It is worth noting that the royal wives were in a trap between the presented luxuries, to which they were obliged and encouraged, and the accusations of vanity directed against them, to which women, in particular, were expected to give in.[3]

This image of the queen and her life was the standard in all the European courts. It is worth emphasising that pursuing all these roles – assuming that the queen taking her first steps at the new court focused the attention of her husband, his family and circles, and usually also the present diplomats – was not easy, especially at the beginning of marriage, when she was getting started at the new royal court. When a young woman got married, she had to leave her family home, usually say goodbye to her loved ones forever, grow into the new place, culture, landscape, weather, scents and smells, get used to different customs, garment designs, and language. These challenges were faced by all European princesses and they did not miss those who left Poland or arrived in the country in order to marry the rulers whom their parents had chosen as husbands, usually wishing for their daughter's happiness, but at the same time pursuing specific political goals. The family's hopes, as well as those of the young couple, were sometimes coinciding, but their implementation varied. There is no doubt that it would be an interesting element – which usually escapes researchers due to the lack of suitable sources – to determine the extent to which women were ready for the roles they were meant to fulfill. The observation of their mothers' behaviour and actions, who performed identical functions, was most certainly not sufficient, and it should be emphasised that there were not too many opportunities in the life of a young girl for such observations; none of them saw their mother taking their first steps at the husband's court. Orientation in the court's life and general rules of manners and etiquette were certainly making it easier for young princesses – brought up in a similar but never the same environment – to enter the new role. However, even the slightest differences in the functioning of the parents' and the husband's court were difficult to accept. In turn, women who came

2 Beem 2020, pp. 154–172.

3 Berry 1994.

from outside of the court circles found it unimaginably challenging to meet the new demands, particularly since they were automatically doomed to a deep dislike by the new circles that were usually showing their superiority in an ostentatious way.

Coming to her husband's court was a challenge to a young woman also because she was usually a figure anticipated by the court community that associated specific hopes with her arrival. The monarch's marriage must have been a decisive change at the court; it was linked with reshuffles necessary in the face of creating the court of his wife or transformations at the court of her predecessor if she was the next wife of this ruler. The fight for the new queen's favours could begin even before her arrival and then continue before her eyes, in front of her, with or without her participation. The new queen's retinue was arriving at the court together with her in order to act as her support, at least in the first phase of growing into the new environment. People who came with her were often burdened with the task of influencing the court and making efforts to reach the ruler's ear, the husband of their mistress. There were also people of a less high-profile who could act more freely; they were usually more experienced and risked less in fulfilling political tasks. This group was usually not welcomed enthusiastically; others wanted to get rid of it almost immediately, explaining it by the need to let the young wife grow into the new environment as soon as possible. In reality, the most important reason was to deprive the queen of support, to prevent her from using the newcomers in the court's game of influence and position, and the "locals" wanted to take a place by her side as soon as possible and win her influence as long as she was poorly oriented in the network of connections in her circles, and she knew little about people surrounding her; there was a greater chance then of having her wrapped in the net of dependencies. If at least part of the retinue with which the queen arrived remained in the new country, it could become an instrument of influence and means of contacting the fatherland or an opportunity for the queen consort's relatives to put pressure on her. On the other hand, the moment these people were leaving the court, there was another breakthrough in shaping the entire balance of power at the court.

Creating the young wife's court usually depended on the king sometimes yielding to his trusted advisor's suggestions, who could aim at lowering the queen's positions and depriving her – as far as possible – of greater importance and influence. To manouevre in this new environment, and in particular to win the husband's attention and trust, was exceptionally difficult; to gain a support group and to face unfriendly people required a great perceptiveness, predicting skills, skillful manner of dealing with often experienced opponents. These challenges could be handled better by women who already had some experience in the political game, but not many had this kind of preparation.

The queen's position at the court, particularly at the beginning, could be based not only on her personal qualities and social competences, but could also depend on the political background created by her connections. If the husband cared about having good relations with his in-laws, if they could have influence on him, support the representative of their own blood, then both the rules as well as his circles had to reckon with the queen, which strengthen her position and influence. However, the royal wife could also be perceived as a foreigner, a dangerous person, accused of spying for the benefit of her relatives, hostile towards her husband's issues.[4] Even giving birth to children did not help the unpopular queens in breaking down those negative opinions, but the lack of offspring and the weak position associated with it only made this matter worse. Hostile and defamatory opinions were often spread by people competing with the queen to gain access to her husband, reluctant to her influence, full of concerns that the faction associated with her would block their own activities.

The aim of this work is to present the queens of the Early Modern Period who lived in varied and complex arrangements of the court as well as family connections. The authors try to present the pressure that was put on queens by their surroundings and people, and the efforts of these women to not succumb to these pressures, to avoid traps, which resulted in submitting to someone else's wishes and goals, even though not all of them knew how to avoid these interplays. Some of the queens tried to create their own networks of family and court connections in order to strengthen their position this way and secure the future of their own family or even the country. Elements of building their own position at the time of getting married and ascending the throne also occur. A considerable role in this narrative was played by the queens' relationships with their husbands, who were also not free from the pressure of their surroundings and arrangements at the court.

There is no doubt that the queens' positions were not easy, even though none of the women presented in this book ruled on her own. Duties imposed on the queen consort, expectations associated with them, and the queen's position in the Polish-Lithuanian Commonwealth were not different from other European countries, but in the face of the throne's eligibility and the monarch's weakening position, her role was also diminishing. Therefore, a question arises whether the removal from power – but not from influences – freed these women from responsibility for the country where they held the throne and whether this responsibility came down only to giving birth to heirs to this throne. This question is linked explicitly to the Polish-Lithuanian Commonwealth as an elective monarchy where the heir to the throne was as important and respected as he was not necessarily needed from the

4 Stafford 1983, pp. 58–59.

legal and political point of view.[5] The rule of the throne's eligibility in Poland was first introduced within the family, and then *virtim*, but it was still important for the royal spouse to give birth to children because it was assumed, at least until the mid-17th century, that the monarch's sons would be the most reliable candidates to the throne.

Undoubtedly, Polish queens had an influence on power and future of the state, or they were suspected of having this possibility, which triggered rivalry and aversion towards them, but they were encouraged to reach for power – even through influencing their husbands – also by their relatives or people from their circles. The active and strong queen was becoming a part of the arrangement of the court, and thus also the political arrangement.[6]

The characters presented in this book are linked by the Polish-Lithuanian Commonwealth, from which they came or to which they were brought by circumstances. Barbara Radziwiłł and Anna Jagiellon were born here and were enthroned here; Marie Leszczyńska, who married the King of France, was also born here. Anna of Austria and Louise-Marie Gonzaga came to Poland to become queens. Marie Casimire de la Grange d'Arquien became the queen thanks to the election of her husband and her granddaughter, Maria Clementina Sobieska, was born in Silesia situated on the border with Poland, and she went to Italy hoping to marry a king who would recover his inheritance; but that is not what happened, and she spent the rest of her life in Rome as *de iure* queen. She was not enthroned as her husband did not win the throne back, but through her own ambitions and political background she relied on, as well as struggles that were shaking the court in exile, she belongs to the group of women presented in this book.[7] They all found friends – if rulers can have any – and supporters; they also all came across people who were adverse personally to them, but also to their husbands and their actions.

Therefore, we wish to present how all the queens, even though linked to the Polish-Lithuanian Commonwealth in different ways, dealt with establishing their position or achieving the goals they set for themselves. It includes both princesses with high-ranked families and background (Anna Jagiellon, Anne of Austria, Louise-Marie Gonzaga) and women who were not born in power circles (Barbara Radziwiłł, Marie Casimire de la Grange d'Arquien, Maria Clementina Sobieska, Marie Leszczyńska), who had to face the challenges that their social elevation caused. The position at the royal court and influence of these women were very diverse, and thus presenting the

---

5 Czapliński 2008, p. 50.

6 Cruz, Suzuki 2009, pp. 3–4.

7 Maria Clementina will soon have her first biography published, which will present not only the history of her life but also uncover numerous misinterpretations about her that are widely present in the historiography of the Stuarts. Skrzypietz, Jujeczka.

family and court arrangements in which they functioned seems to be an important element of their biographies.

Barbara Radziwiłł (1523–1551), the representative of the Lithuanian aristocracy, a widow of her first husband, Stanislovas Goštautas, met Sigismund II Augustus at the time when he already had the crown which he had received as a child when his father had still been alive. When they met, he was still married to Elisabeth of Austria, who soon died. Barbara became the Jagiellonian monarch's wife in the atmosphere of scandal.[8] Their secret wedding forced the king – when he took over independent power after the death of his father, Sigismund I the Old – to the long-lasting efforts to have the marriage recognized and to have Barbara crowned.[9] No one can answer the question to what extent the difficult entry into the role of a royal spouse and dislike, which she encountered, damaged Barbara's health and contributed to her premature death. The fact that – being sick as she was – she did not give her husband any offspring also seriously diminished her position at the court. Agnieszka Januszek-Sieradzka presents the process of the royal spouse's growing into the role of the queen. The short marriage of only four years with the Jagiellonian monarch let her strengthen neither her position nor her influence, all the more so, because the majority of this time was dedicated to the king's fight for the coronation of his beloved wife. Barbara became a victim of her subjects' dislike, who deemed her unworthy of this elevation. Sigismund II Augustus's persistence resulted in her coronation taking place six months before her death when she was already very ill. Married to the monarch, Barbara was the object of pressure and demands from her relatives, who expected her to become a tool in their hands and a pathway to achieving their ambitions and political plans. Meanwhile, the king highly appreciated his wife's inactivity. The article uncovers contradictions in which the queen was entangled and her circle's reactions to her behaviour.

Anna Jagiellon (1523–1596) should have become a wife of a foreign ruler, similarly to her three sisters, but neither her parents nor her brother found time to find her a husband, even though her younger sister, Catherine, did get married. After the death of her brother, Sigismund II Augustus, Anna had to take care of her own future. Unmarried for many years and living isolated from the political life, she – as the last representative of the Jagiellonian dynasty in Poland – was of interest to the noblemen who wanted to secure her future and wealth. This moment opened up for her the opportunity to pursue broader activities at home and abroad. The issue of taking over the inheritance of her mother, Bona Sforza, and the execution of her siblings' wills were the subjects of her efforts. However, the elections required much greater efforts, and Anna became a participant in the political games during

8 Januszek-Sieradzka 2017, p. 29.

9 Marchwińska 2011, pp. 484–499.

three of them. The aging maiden hoped twice to get married, first to Henry Valois and then to Stephen Báthory, and it was the latter who got the crown together with her hand.[10] Anna turned fifty at that time, and even though her health was not bad, she could not have any children.[11] Agnieszka Pawłowska-Kubik proved that Anna – having practically no political experience – managed to get involved in wide-scale activities and create a network of connections that served to carry out her plans. She also knew how to find influential allies, skilfully seek for their help, and remind them of their obligations. She energetically supported her relatives in the political fight, working on their marriages. She consistently and successfully worked on placing her nephew, Sigismund III Vasa, on the Polish throne.

Anne of Austria (1573–1598) was the child of Archduke Charles, the younger brother of Emperor Maximilian II. Her marriage to Sigismund III Vasa was set up by Anna Jagiellon, who started the talks to win the archduchess' hand for her nephew, even though the final word allegedly belonged to the fiancé who liked the portrait of young Anne.[12] Her marriage, arrival to Poland, and coronation did not differ from the accepted norms. Anne gave birth to a few children, and her son, Władysław, was chosen the king after his father's death. It can be stated that her short life and marriage was an exemplary model of a queen's biography, which does not mean that she did not come across problems after becoming the ruler's wife and that she did not have to learn her new role. Young Anne was brought to Poland by her mother, Archduchess Maria Anna of Bavaria, an energetic woman who was successfully pursuing her own political plans and who wanted to have an influence on her daughter. This was meant to be achieved through leaving trusted people in the Polish queen's circles, through whom she could contact her daughter, but also get detailed news about the situation at the Polish court. Anne herself was to be a source of information as she was obliged to write to her mother regularly. As a result, Maria Anna of Bavaria could follow the events and try to influence the queen's attitude. Thus, she encouraged her to take actions beneficial to her own views or the Habsburgs' interests. Aleksandra Barwicka-Makula traces the family letters, uncovering the archduchess' role in both leading to her daughter's marriage to the King of Poland and indicating that Anne was to become an intermediary in her mother's efforts to make Sigismund III act in accordance with the plans of his in-laws. The author emphasises that even though only remnants of the family letters survived, they are still a vast source of knowledge on the relationship between the archduchess and her daughter and son-in-law.

---

10 Pawłowska-Kubik 2019, p. 236.

11 Bogucka 2009.

12 Barwicka-Makula 2019, p. 329.

Louise-Marie Gonzaga (1611–1667) was born as Marie, and the name Louise was taken by her before her departure to Poland. Her life in France was marked by participating in political and matrimonial scandals, similarly to Anna, her sister.[13] She was suggested as the wife of Władysław IV Vasa twice, and the second time this not-so-young, already thirty-four-year-old princess became his wife just to become a widow three years later and to marry his brother, the next King of Poland, John II Casimir. Louise-Marie's asset was her large dowry and a considerable amount of cash that came from selling her French properties, which she brought to Poland; she also knew the court's customs and brought with her a group of young ladies whom she married off very well in order to use them in the political game, which provoked opposition against "the rule of a skirt". The efforts of the queen, who was openly reaching for power and scheming to implement her political plans, exposed her to the nobility's dislike.[14] The catastrophic situation of the Polish-Lithuanian Commonwealth in the mid-17th century resulted in the queen searching for allies abroad and introducing the *vivente rege* election, which was to strengthen the Polish monarch's position. Two children born in the queen's second marriage died, and so plans were made to enthrone her adopted niece, Anne Henriette, and her husband, Duke d'Enghien.[15] A thread of connection between the queen and his father, Louis de Bourbon, Prince of Condé, was exceptionally complicated and linked many people who mediated the contacts between Warsaw, Chantilly, and Paris. Damien Mallet presented how complex and strong the network of connections linking Louise-Marie with France was, but he also included problems of people involved in it, first and foremost the tensions arising among these people, particularly in the face of challenges engendered by the double dependence on both the queen and the Conti family.

Marie Casimire de la Grange d'Arquien (1641?–1716) came from the poor French nobility, and she arrived in the Polish-Lithuanian Commonwealth together with Louise-Marie. Thanks to the queen and in accordance with her plans, she married John Sobieski, who was quickly climbing his career ladder. Brought up in the queen's political "school", she did not shy away from taking part in intrigues and making efforts to have a French candidate enthroned, in accordance with the queen's intentions. However, the opposite happened, and the throne was taken by Michał Korybut Wiśniowiecki, and Marie Casimire – even though her husband was the leader of the anti-king opposition – sought acceptance at the court, and thus she was accused of using female tricks against the king.[16] She also joined the political game during the following election supporting her husband's candidature, and she

13 Skrzypietz 2019, pp. 68,76–77.

14 Mallet 2017, pp. 455–469.

15 Libiszowska 1985, pp. 55–67.

16 Matyasik 2011, p. 35.

was enthroned together with him. She knew the court, she had a great experience in manoeuvring the pathways of the court's arrangements, but her humble birth status and willingness to get involved in the political activities triggered a widespread resentment. Together with her husband, she had to fight for her coronation, the right which she was denied, similarly to their children born before the election who were denied the titles of royal descendants.[17] She managed to overcome these obstacles, but her husband's reign was taking place amid fierce fighting against the opposition. It was Marie Casimire's ambition to preserve power in the hand of her children. However, it turned out that the changing political situation and the lack of a strong family and political background made this task very difficult. Therefore, the queen decided to create a network of ties based on marriages of her relatives with the most prominent families of the Polish-Lithuanian Commonwealth. Dominika Rychel-Mantur indicates that the effort to strengthen the position of the Sobieski family through John III's relatives and the queen's siblings brought from France turned out to be a failed attempt, and the fiasco of these efforts seems to reside in the weakened position of the Polish ruler, intensifying in the second half of the 17th century,

Maria Clementina Sobieska (1701–1735) was the granddaughter of John III Sobieski and Marie Casimire. She was born in Oława, where her father, James Sobieski, took refuge after he had lost the election in 1697. John III Sobieski's sons did not sit on the Polish throne, but they constantly tried to participate in the international political game, believing that they will win the Polish crown. However, that is not what happened, and the family of John III lost its significance, even though legends about its wealth circulated around Europe. Through her mother, Hedwig Elisabeth of Palatinate-Neuburg, Maria Clementina was related to families who held many European thrones. Maria Clementina's asset was her youth, giving her hope that she would have sons; she was chosen as the future wife of James Stuart, the English king *de iure*, who tried to keep the support of his advocates by giving them the potential heir to the throne of the Stuarts' blood and royal rights. Improving his situation thanks to his wife's relatives and repairing the finances was very important for the exiled king who had just settled in Rome. However, James Stuart's enemies remained alert, and Maria Clementina – at the order of the emperor, Charles VI, who acted in the interests of George I, King of England – was confined in Innsbruck, from where she was freed through a ruse.[18] There was no great retinue that would lead her to the husband, although when she reached Rome, she was welcomed by the cardinals and the pope. Her husband did not wait for her since, once again, he tried to recover the lost throne. The small circles of

17 Komaszyński 1983.

18 Miller 1968.

the Jacobite immigrants were shaken by fierce arguments. Sobieska joined these conflicts fighting for her own position. The payout of her dowry turned out to be difficult, and her connections did not bring James Stuart back to the throne, which diminished her influence. She gave birth to a son, fulfilling the task of the king's spouse, but despite this, her position at the court in exile was waning because the hope to return to the throne was increasingly declining. Efforts of the monarch's favourites who tried to block Maria Clementina's influence on her husband resulted in tensions between the royal couple. The escalating conflict resulting from the fights of the court's factions prompted Sobieska to act against the favourites and the decisions of the king who – according to her – succumbed to them.

Marie Leszczyńska (1703–1768) was born in the family of a Polish nobleman and together with her father's election – carried out at the request of the Swedish king, Charles XII – she was elevated to the position of a princess, but this did not mean the actual advancement since the political turmoil and the great northern war forced her family to exile. Internment and then Charles XII's death deprived her father, King Stanisław, of influence, and the family's financial situation was also hopeless. Despite small hope for an excellent marriage in the absence of dowry and influential political background, Marie was relatively well educated, but she had no chance to experience the functioning of the royal court with all its complexities. Due to conflicts shaking the circles of young Louis XV and changes in the French government, it was decided that a princess should be found, who could quickly give birth to an heir to the throne. Marie Leszczyńska was selected, but the faction which brought her to the throne also expected to win the monarch's favours through her mediation.[19] The Polish princess had no support in the form of a royal family who could benefit from her influence; she ended up in Versailles, in the environment marked by a long tradition of the court and etiquette. Not used to life at the court, Marie found herself in a net of dynastic and personal dependencies. Giving birth to sons and many daughters did not strengthen her position, and the presence of Louis XV's influential mistresses meant that the efforts to win the influence of the king's wife became even more difficult. Katarzyna Kuras presents Marie Leszczyńska in the net of intrigues and rivalries that surrounded her, and she tries to explain the reasons for the queen's weak position at the court, illustrating the picture of her loneliness in the face of the lack of family and political background since Leszczyńska did not have those at her disposal. This example indicates that even though personal predispositions and skills could provide the queen's influence, they could, in fact, help only to a small extent; for the origins, family, and political background – which assisted the royal wife in strengthening her position – were much more important.

19 Kuras 2018, pp. 44–51.

Bibliography

Barwicka-Makula 2019 = Aleksandra Barwicka-Makula, *Od wrogości do przyjaźni: Habsburgowie austriaccy wobec Polski w latach 1587–1592*, Wydawnictwo Uniwersytetu Śląskiego, Katowice 2019.

Beem 2020 = Charles Beem, *Queenship in Early Modern Europe*, Red Globe Press, London 2020.

Berry 1994 = Christopher I. Berry, *The Idea of Luxury. A Conceptual and Historical Investigation*, Cambridge University Press, Cambridge 1994.

Bogucka 2009 = Maria Bogucka, *Anna Jagiellonka*, Zakład Narodowy im. Ossolińskich, Wrocław 2009.

Cruz, Suzuki 2009 = Anne J. Cruz, Mihoko Suzuki, Introduction. [In:] *The Rule of Women in Early Modern Europe*, ed. Anne J. Cruz, Mihoko Suzuki, University of Illinois Press, Urbana - Chicago 2009.

Czapliński 2008 = Władysław Czapliński, *Władysław IV i jego czasy*, Towarzystwo Autorów i Wydawców Prac Naukowych "Universitas", Cracow 2008.

Januszek-Sieradzka 2017 = Agnieszka Januszek-Sieradzka, *Królowa Barbara Radziwiłłówna w dworskim mikroświecie*, Wydawnictwo KUL, Lublin 2017.

Komaszyński 1983 = Michał Komaszyński, *Maria Kazimiera d'Arquien Sobieska królowa Polski (1641–1716)*, Wydawnictwo Literackie, Cracow 1983.

Kuras 2018 = Katarzyna Kuras, *Dwór królowej Marii Leszczyńskiej: ludzie, pieniądze, wpływy*, Towarzystwo Wydawnicze "Historia Iagellonica", Cracow 2018.

Libiszowska 1985 = Zofia Libiszowska, *Królowa Ludwika Maria*, Zamek Królewski, Warsaw 1985.

Mallet 2017 = Damien Mallet, "Ce pays de Cocagne oû les choses changent si souvent". *Le regard de Pierre des Noyers, secrétaire de la reine Louise-Marie, sur la Pologne de son temps (1645–1693)*, Toruń 2017 (typescript in Library of UMK, Toruń).

Marchwińska 2011 = Agnieszka Marchwińska, *Starania Zygmunta Augusta o uznanie Barbary Radziwiłłówny w Koronie*. [In:] *"A Pomerania ad ultimas terras". Studia ofiarowane Barbarze Popielas-Szultce w sześćdziesiątą piątą rocznicę urodzin i czterdziestolecie pracy naukowej*, ed. Jarosław Sochacki, Agnieszka Teterycz-Puzio, Wydawnictwo Naukowe Akademii Pomorskiej, Słupsk 2011.

Matyasik 2011 = Joanna Matyasik, *Obóz polityczny króla Michała Korybuta Wiśniowieckiego*, Wydawnictwo Neriton: Instytut Historii PAN, Warsaw 2011.

Miller 1968 = Peggy Miller, *Żona dla Pretendenta, rzecz o Marii Klementynie Sobieskiej*, tłum. Anna Przedpełska-Trzeciakowska, „Czytelnik", Warsaw 1968.

Pawłowska-Kubik 2019 = Agnieszka Pawłowska-Kubik, *Epistolografia i historia medycyny: problemy zdrowotne w korespondencji Anny Jagiellonki*. [In:] *Epistolografia w dawnej Rzeczypospolitej, T. VIII: Literatura, historia, język*, red. Piotr Borek, Marceli Olma, Marcin Piątek, Collegium Columbinum, Cracow 2019.

Skrzypietz 2019 = Aleksandra Skrzypietz, *Franciszek Ludwik, książę de Conti – „obrany król Polski". Saga rodu Kondeuszów*, Wydawnictwo Uniwersytetu Śląskiego, Katowice 2019.

Skrzypietz, Jujeczka = Aleksandra Skrzypietz, Stanisław Jujeczka, *Maria Klementyna Sobieska królowa i służebnica Boża* (w druku Wydawnictwo Uniwersytetu Śląskiego, Katowice).

Stafford 1983 = Pauline Stafford, *Queens, Concubines and Dowagers. The King's Wife in the Early Middle Ages*, Leicester University Press, London-Washington (DC) 1983.

Agnieszka Januszek-Sieradzka

Queen Barbara Radziwiłł in a Web of Contradictory Expectations*

In Memory of My Beloved Parents

Abstract:
Barbara Radziwiłł (1523–1551), a second wife of King Sigismund II Augustus (1520–1572, reign from 1548), spent only four years with her husband, of which only six months as a crowned queen (7 December 1550 – 8 May 1551). Due to the backdrop of this unequal and socially unacceptable marriage between the monarch and the Lithuanian magnate, a widow of a strained reputation, this short period of time excellently shows the process of "becoming the queen". It was difficult and fraught with traps even in favourable conditions, but under the circumstances Barbara got involved, it became particularly difficult and complex. The king's beloved wife, but an unwanted queen, struggled at the royal court in Cracow with numerous problems, facing also one which put her under the pressure of contradicting expectations of people closest to her – her husband and the Radziwiłł family that dreamt of strengthening and expanding their influence. In Sigismund Augustus' eyes, one of Barbara's major assets was her lack of interest in the state or public affairs. The queen did not want to lose this asset. What moved her husband's heart towards her, alienated her from all others who wanted to reach the monarch's favour through her. The queen's attitude was the source of annoyance for the power-hungry Radziwiłł relatives who – although they could rely on the monarch's favour anyway – attempted to extend their sphere of influence and benefits, taking advantage of having their family's representative enthroned and constantly pressuring her, making requests, and indicating a route for their implementation. How did the queen – being hardly able to find herself in the royal court' reality – navigate in this web of contradictory expectations? This is what this article addresses.

* The article was written using materials prepared as part of the 2018/29/B/HS3/00907 project: Polish Courtier at the Royal Courts of the Jagiellons and Elective Kings: Rank, Value System, Role Model (Dworzanin polski na dworze Jagiellonów i królów elekcyjnych. Pozycja, system wartości, wzorzec osobowy), financed by the National Science Centre.

There were, in fact, three expectations of a Queen in Poland, common to all the members of public life, both in the mid-16th century as well as earlier and later periods: she was to give birth to an heir to the throne (the Jagiellonian elective monarchy also required successors), she should appear publicly in order to emphasise her husband's position and wealth, and it was her duty to also set an example of a good life as an exemplary Christian, wife, and mother, and she was to emotionally link the subjects with the monarch and monarchy.[1] It was also perfectly clear and natural that the queen would not get involved in politics or any state affairs, leaving these matters in an exclusive and undisputed domain of her husband, the king.[2] While the queen's obligations were of a universal dimension in Early Modern Europe, for they were similar regardless of the latitude or the political and institutional shape of the country, the socio-cultural landscape into which the queen had to fit after her arrival to her husband's homeland and where she had to fulfill these obligations, tended to be exceedingly different, also from what her country of origin had made her used to. In 1380 Leopold III, Duke of Austria, brought his future daughter-in-law, Jadwiga of Anjou, who was only a few years old at that time, to the court in Vienna not only to ensure the terms of the marriage agreement with his son were honoured, but also for the young Hungarian to grow into the Habsburg tradition, culture, and customs.[3] A queen's skill to effectively and advantageously navigate through this maze of often contradictory expectations was a real challenge – a highly difficult art of playing many pianofortes at once, requiring vigilance, foresight, caution, and a constant calculation of profits and losses.

A Lithuanian magnate, Barbara Radziwiłł (1523–1551, queen from 7 December 1550), a widow with a terrible reputation[4], in 1547 she became the second wife of Sigismund II Augustus (1520–1572, reigned from 1548) after a scandalous romance, in secret, without the knowledge and consent of her parents and the royal council, in the face of a hurricane opposition from Polish political elites, as well as extensive masses of nobility.[5] Barbara became the wife of the Polish heir to the throne in unconventional circumstance, and this atypicality somehow turned out into a trademark, or perhaps a heavy burden, of her short life by the side of Sigismund Augustus. The husband in love tied to provide his beloved with as many rituals as possible – typical of the entire dynastic Europe – of changing her status from an

1 Mrówczyńska 1983; Beem 2020, pp. 154–172.

2 Cf. Brzezińska 1999; Beem 2020, pp. 158–163.

3 CDHung., IX, vol. 5, pp. 376–380; Przybyszewski 1975, pp. 109–110.

4 On the origins, family, and the first childless marriage between Barbara and Stanislovas Goštautas (1507–1542), voivode of Nowogród i Trakai, whom she married in 1537, and on the reputation of the future queen, more broadly in: Kuchowicz, 1989, pp. 8–22, 61–74; Ragauskienė 1999, pp. 39–85; Kołodziejczyk 2015, pp. 361–374.

5 Kuchowicz 1989, pp. 97–125; Sucheni–Grabowska 1996, pp. 122–133.

unmarried woman to a wife, from a royal consort to a crowned queen. The process of "becoming the queen" did not go according to the accepted and expected norms. Barbara took part in a series of ceremonies which were secret (getting married), incomplete and postponed (travel to Poland, inauguration and presentation at the Cracow's castle), and substitutive (quasi-wedding games in Niepołomice near Cracow).[6] Determined Sigismund Augustus provided Barbara also with a substitute of his personal rituals of separation and reception ("rituels de séparation et d'accueil"), facilitating a woman's adaptation to a new legal and social situation, arranging her almost a classical "le voyage de la jeune mariée".[7] Despite the husband's efforts and carefully staged ceremonies, Barbara Radziwiłł could not count on a realistic welcome to her new family and to a new royal court. The royal consort found out about it in a palpable and painful way the minute she was brought to the rooms intended for her. In order for Barbara to take the rooms, it was first necessary to break the door down that had been locked up tight by Sigismund Augustus' mother, Bona Sforza (1594–1557), who – not wanting to share the Wawel residence with her unrecognized daughter-in-law, had ostentatiously left Wawel and went to Warsaw.[8]

As aptly noted by Grażyna Rutkowska, a queen could usually recognize "the social expectations towards her because she was constantly meeting the representatives of various circles both at the royal court and outside of it (royal family, clergymen, university scholars, and other guests). She could shape and perfect her image under their influence".[9] This seemingly universal statement did not apply in the case of queen Barbara Radziwiłł. She came to the Cracow's royal court with no knowledge, skills, and competencies typical of women who were being prepared to become a ruler's wife since childhood, as well as no experience which allowed to get oneself acquainted with practices of living at the summits of power. The majority of the representatives of those "various circles", apart from those – initially only few – whom Sigismund Augustus managed to convince to support – or at least staying neutral towards – the new queen, did not expect her to perfect her image under their influence. The only thing expected of Radziwiłł was to immediately and permanently remove herself from Sigismund Augustus' life, from the Cracow's royal court, from Poland. It was not an expectation explicitly directed to the unwanted queen, but in different forms and from different sides addressed to her husband, a sovereign, to take steps to end this relationship as soon as possible, even against the wife's will, but with universal support. Those who were traditionally supposed to influence the queen to have her shape and improve her image did everything

6 Targosz 2007; Januszek-Sieradzka 2017a, pp. 133–151.

7 Muir 1997, pp. 32–39; Coester 2011; Van Gennep 2019, pp. 116–145; Kosior 2019, pp. 23–45; Pastrnak 2020; Januszek-Sieradzka 2017a, pp. 133–151.

8 Elementa, XXXVIII, p. 111.

9 Rutkowska 2014, p. 234.

so that Barbara Radziwiłł would not only not become a crowned queen but also stop being the king's wife. Sigismund Augustus' mother and sister ostentatiously took a stand against young Jagiellon's choice. Bona – always thinking and acting in terms of the dynasty's and national interest's wellbeing, and never shrinking from subordinating all the matters to them – began to act energetically against his only son's marriage, hoping that he would come to his senses under pressure and end this "unfortunate and pathetic marriage".[10] It should be remembered that in this case, she was hurt not only as a queen but also as a mother who suddenly lost influence over her beloved only son who was ready to sacrifice his long and close relationship with his mother for the love of another woman. The old queen did not want to accept the new one. She wanted to remove her and win back the exclusive filial feelings.[11] Towards the end of 1548, when Sigismund Augustus was fighting to have his marriage recognised at the Diet session in Piotrków, the widowed queen was to offer her son a hundred thousand zloty and all the estates in Lithuania in exchange for sending Barbara Radziwiłł away.[12] Church and lay dignitaries in the senate, like i.e. Jan Tęczyński (1484–1552), the governor of Sandomierz, who were rebuked for not complying properly with obligations towards the young king, stated that "they would prefer to see Turkish Suleiman in Cracow than to see this one [Barbara Radziwiłł – A.J.-S.] as a queen in Poland".[13] During the Diet session, the deputies – in their eloquent speeches which urged the king to "leave the marriage" – combined the postulates of legal and institutional nature with a genuine concern for the rank of the dynasty and state, and in the end, in a spectacularly dramatic gesture, "they knelt, wiping their tears away many times, openly expressing a sincere sorrow".[14] There were also those who did not shrink from propagating an absurd gossip that Primate Mikołaj Dzierzgowski (c. 1490–1559) supposedly stated that "if some kind of sin was to fall on the king due to this split up, he would divide it between all heads in Poland for the public good".[15] The nobility was even willing to voluntarily put taxes on themselves for the purpose of Barbara's financial security until the end of her life, as long as this life was far from the Polish monarch.

---

10 Listy polskie 2001, pp. 1–2, 10–11.

11 Bogucka 2004, pp. 142–145; cf. Watanabe-O'kelly 2017, pp. 25–36.

12 Elementa, XLIV, p. 26; Sucheni-Grabowska 1996, p. 164 and n. 12; Ferenc 2014, p. 302. On the proceedings of the Diet session and the king's efforts to have his marriage to Barbara Radziwiłł recognized more broadly in: Sucheni-Grabowska 1996, pp. 150–166; Marchwińska 2001, pp. 484–499.

13 Citation from: Szujski 1886, p. 121.

14 Diariusz 1548, p. 207; Elementa, XXXVIII, pp. 74–77; Januszek-Sieradzka 2014, pp. 172–176; Kosior 2019, pp. 126–136.

15 Orzechowski 1854, p. 24; Pociecha 1947, p. 58.

If these expectations – directed more to Sigismund Augustus to send away his universally unaccepted wife than to Barbara to leave her husband and Poland, which was unwelcoming to her – ever reached her then with a significantly weakened power. Sigismund Augustus tried to protect his wife from gossips, but solutions applied by him sometimes worked like a double-edged sword. Wanting to shelter Barbara from the malevolent members of the royal court, but more broadly from the representatives of the nobility associated with the royal court, he ordered Barbara's extensive isolation. On the one hand, this clearly separated her from evil looks and evil tongues, but on the other hand, it seriously hindered for her to get to know this new world, to find herself in it, and finally to adapt to the new role. It would be difficult to assume that in the royal court's circles, even the most carefully selected and the most strictly controlled, the queen's ears did not come across opinions of her new family and new subjects who demanded her separation from the king. However, while Sigismund Augustus' was a shield protecting her from direct contact with them, she had to be more independent when facing immediate contact with peoples' expectations.

The circles the queen had contact with most often was her female court, an environment inherently conflicted, and – when it came to Barbara – unfriendly, where the young queen, despite her husband's efforts to arrange it, found neither support nor kindness.[16] Nevertheless, with the help of her spouse, Radziwiłł managed to meet the most important expectations from the ladies-in-waiting and their noble families, i.e. to take care of their advantageous marriages.[17]

Members of her male court also had expectations of the young queen, but these were far more serious than an advantageous marriage. The matter of these hopes was more complicated because it did not refer to the internal issues of the royal court but the public and state affairs; meanwhile, the queen did not show the smallest interest in them. Her attempts at offering patronage to the state offices or church dignities, confirmed by the sources, are rare. The members of Radziwiłł's court quickly realised the fact that their service for the queen, even after surviving the first, exceptionally difficult period associated with the social ostracism, did not give any real chances for quick promotions, financial gains, or even less spectacular, but gradual building up of one's position.

The queen's Hofmeister, Stanisław Maciejowski (1500–1563), and her secretary, Stanisław Koszucki (died 1559), unequivocally assessed that instead of respect and devotion to serving Barbara, her behaviour resulted in resentment and bitterness.

---

16 Marchwińska 2001; Januszek-Sieradzka 2017a, pp. 23–56.

17 Despite misunderstandings and grievances in the female circle, and only three year period when the court functioned, as many as 9 – out of her 14 – ladies-in-waiting found husbands during their stay at the royal court, and 3 maids-in-waiting from Barbara's court also entered into matrimonies (Marchwińska 2008, pp. 136, 142–144; Januszek-Sieradzka 2017a, pp. 30–32).

They both expressed an opinion that the queen could have and should have made an effort to try for the kindness of "common people" and, through her relevant conduct, could have easily won it, while if she did not take care of good behaviour and she did not try for the subjects' love, she would bring upon herself not only trouble but also God's punishment. Barbara's image emerging from Stanisław Koszucki's letters, a trusted and friendly person, was very far from what her officials and courtiers expected of her as queen. In August of 1549, nearly begging Barbara's brother, Mikołaj "the Red" Radziwiłł (c. 1515–1584), for intervention on his own and Hofmeister's behalf, he expressed the queen's image as excessively condescending and disregarding everyone in her circles, having the royal court's etiquette and customs for nothing, being impertinent, haughty, and despising people. The queen's secretary directly warned that Barbara's inappropriate behaviour towards people who were seeking her support was very harmful to her and negatively influenced opinion about her among the courtiers.[18] He had no doubt that the lack of response to the expectations coming from her closest royal circles was quickly increasing the number of people unfriendly towards her.

It is difficult not to notice the young queen's complicated situation. On the one hand, one of her major strengths in the eyes of Sigismund Augustus was her lack of interest in the state or public affairs, which was manifested, i.e. by this specific reluctance to get involved in undertaking favouritism measures. The queen did not want to lose this asset. On the other hand, what turned her husband's heart towards her was also alienating her from everyone who wanted to reach the king's favours through her. Sigismund Augustus must have realised how much her image suffered because of not using one of the few attributes she had at her disposal to win over the subjects' affection and respect. He never gave her a chance to present herself as to the nobility as an effective advocate. Not without a reason, the royal secretary wrote that "there are more poor than rich in Poland – if everyone put their trust in her, one for his brother, the other for his brother-in-law, the third one for himself, they would wish her even more Lord's love, and they would ask God's favour for her (…)."[19] He also added that it was not only a matter of winning over the influential nobility elites but also the „commoners", who in their masses that would love the queen, would force the change of attitude of those placed higher in the social ranks.

It would be a mistake to believe that the queen never wanted or, even more so, could not help a courtier asking for patronage, although – and contrary to the universal opinion about Barbara's almost unlimited influence over her husband – her pleas not always meant that the matter was settled in accordance with the petitioner's wishes. Despite Barbara's pleas, the refusal was extended to her court's

18 Listy polskie 2001, pp. 363–364, 368–373.

19 Listy polskie 2001, p. 374.

Hofmeister, Stanisław Maciejowski, who tried to get – with the queen's help – the castellany of Sandomierz in the spring of 1548. Sigismund Augustus could not grant his wife's request since he had already promised this office to someone else, but he promised to take into account Maciejowki's merits and "not to shun" him at the next vacancy.[20] The most telling example of Radziwiłł's support, although finished only in partial success, was the case of the efforts made by her chancellor, Jerzy Podlodowski (c. 1515–1555), to get the Cracow's bishopric. Radziwiłł did not refuse to support her official. Barbara's request, strengthened by her brother's support, brought the expected result and Podlodowski achieved Sigismund Augustus' promise to receive the bishop's seat in Cracow.[21] Even though a confluence of unfavourable circumstances did not let Podlodowski to take the coveted dignity in the end,[22] it can be clearly seen that the young queen did not always evade the efforts to seek promotions for her officials. In the royal court's social network and the complicated network of political agreements, it is possible to assume that Barbara knew how to recognize a situation in which her pleas were consistent with or at least not contrary to the king's plans, and not shy away from winning this way the gratitude of people connected with those cases.

Expectations of and plans for Barbara were expressed by her family members, particularly by the most politically talented of the Radziwiłłs – Mikołaj "the Black" Radziwiłł (1515–1565), her cousin, and the queen's own bother, Mikołaj "the Red" Radziwiłł, who cooperated with him. The young Radziwiłłs started to climb the ladder of a political, clerical, and financial career already at the times of Sigismund Augustus' reign in 1544–1548, but the king's marriage with the representative of their family opened up completely new perspectives for them.[23] The Radziwiłłs' expectations of Barbara were great and far-reaching, opening up a chance for their implementation was not possible without overcoming the general aversion, strengthening and consolidating her position, and convincingly and quickly making her find herself in the role of the king's wife and queen. An experienced and far-seeing politician like Mikołaj "the Black" knew this very well, and if Barbara's coronation was to take place, it was necessary "to get involved in the ruling, but first of all to endear peoples' love and friendship". However, he expected above all the change in Barbara's attitude towards her husband, which he thought was too haughty

---

20 Listy polskie 2001, p. 34. The king kept his word to Barbara – after her death, in 1553, Stanisław Maciejowski received the long-awaited castellany of Sandomierz – Dworzaczek 1974.

21 Górnicki 2003, p. 45.

22 Regarding this matter, Sigismund Augustus gave in to Archbishop Mikołaj Dzierzgowski, who was opposed to entrusting the bishopric to the canon who would owe his promotion only to the king. Dzierzgowski threatened the king with departure, which – in view of his wife's upcoming coronation – the monarch did not want to allow (Górnicki 2003, pp. 44–47; Gołąbek 2012, pp. 198–201).

23 Ferenc 2009.

and lacking the necessary humility.[24] On the one hand, the Radziiwiłłs commented, sometimes in indiscriminate words, Barbara's careless – in their opinion – behaviour and erroneous arrangement of her marital relations. On the other hand – the frequent and insistent expectations addressed her way to act as an intermediary in dealing with the Radziwiłłs' affairs could not help her. It seems that Barbara, fundamentally reluctant to pleading her husband for anything, also for the members of her own family, developed over time a specific practice in handling such matters. She redirected these requests to her husband without taking the side of those seeking favour, and often she was also buying her time and was delaying the presentation of the matters to the king. The tactic of resorting to the royal husband's authority and will was best practiced in the case of exceptionally frequent and insistent requests by Mikołaj "the Red" Radziwiłł.[25] Barbara's quick death did not allow to fully take advantage of the chance the Radziwiłłs saw in her marriage to Sigismund Augustus, and particularly in the coronation which – after many attempts and in spite of the opposition of the nobility's elites – was finally carried out in December 1550, half a year before the queen's death.[26] Barbara's death did not turn out to be the end of expectations towards her because she could serve her family also in her life after death. Radziwiłłs tried many times to convince Sigismund Augustus to bury Barbara in Cracow and not in Vilnius as was her wish, arguing that she should rest "among the bodies of other kings".[27] They were both concerned about holding on to the dominant position in Lithuania and the previous political significance of the House of Radziwiłł after the death of Barbara – the queen.[28]

In this net of expectations that were contradictory, impossible to fulfill, or completely indifferent for Barbara, only Sigismund Augustus' expectations were the subject of her constant and authentic concern. Not only in the opinion of the ordinary members of the royal court, but also the influential officials, Barbara was supposedly notorious for taking her husband away from the public matters, and it was a universal expectation of her to not occupy too much of the king's time

24 Listy polskie 2001, pp. 108–109.

25 Listy polskie 2001, pp. 249, 380–381; Januszek-Sieradzka 2017a, pp. 46–51; cf. Ferenc 2006.

26 Januszek-Sieradzka 2017b, pp. 153–159. Sigismund Augustus probably remembered the history of Helena of Moscow (1476–1513), the wife of Alexander Jagiellon (1461–1506), recalled in 1548 at the Sejm session with undisguised contempt by the castellan of Kalisz, Marcin Zborowski (Diariusz 1548, p. 215). He was also aware that the resignation from Helena's coronation – due to the decision to remain in the Orthodox Church – excluded her permanently from full participation in both family and public life. Despite the lack of the crown, Helena was treated in Poland with dignity and royal honours; however, this by no means changed the actual situation that there was only one Queen in Poland under the sceptre of Alexander – Elisabeth of Austria (c. 1436–1505), the widow of Casimir IV of Poland (1427–1492) (Rutkowska 2014, pp. 230–233; Mickūnaitė 2017).

27 Listy polskie 2004, p. 161; Januszek-Sieradzka 2010.

28 Listy polskie 2004, pp. 160–162; Sucheni-Grabowska 1996, pp. 268–269; Ferenc 2008, p. 158.

and attention. Sigismund Augustus' expectation was quite the opposite. In love with Barbara Radziwiłł, the monarch seemed to be thoroughly satisfied with her very presence by his side. If he did not accept then he certainly tolerated her behaviour which gave other members of the life at court a cause for concern; he did not demand from his wife to adapt to the Wawel's etiquette and ceremonial, flexibly adapting them to her (just as the coronation ceremony was changed for her)[29] or simply ignoring her behaviour that was inconsistent with the custom and not expecting any changes (like her being notoriously late). Unlike the majority of spouses of European monarchs, Barbara did not face the necessity of cutting herself off from her family circles. While it was considered natural and necessary to send back the queen's countrymen to her family court as soon as possible after the wedding,[30] Barbara was not only in constant and close contact with the members of her family, but Sigismund Augustus made attempts to even provide her with the presence of a companion from the closest family circles at the Wawel court.[31] Apart from love, the Jagiellonian monarch required from his wife two things – not getting involved in the state affairs and giving him children. Barbara fully met her husband's expectation to stay indifferent to political matters, and she tried to fulfill the king's dream of having a son. It seems that Sigismund Augustus not only hoped for offspring from his marriage to Barbara, but he also expected it at least twice. Barbara Radziwiłł thought she was pregnant in the autumn of 1547 and had a miscarriage in November that year.[32] She was supposedly expecting a child for the second time in 1548, but also this pregnancy ended with losing the child in May of June that year. Regardless of whether Barbara was pregnant or what she thought were the signs of pregnancy were, in fact, the first symptoms of the developing cancer,[33] and whether Sigismund Augustus able to beget a child or not,[34] it was their mutual expectation to have offspring together. Barbara, who was very eager to meet her husband's hopes, was undergoing special infertility treatments, which included taking some mixtures which – as some scholars assume – could have caused the development of the disease.[35] Desperate attempts to become a mother of the royal heir and successor were, however, going thoroughly against the tide of peoples' expectations. This was a completely unique situation in which the so-far childless king, the last representative of a respected and distinguished dynasty, was

29 BN, ms III.6614, tab. 173–175v; Kutrzeba 1911; Januszek-Sieradzka 2017a, pp. 153–178; Januszek-Sieradzka 2017b.

30 Coester 2011; Sypek 2009.

31 Listy polskie 2001, pp. 339–340; Januszek-Sieradzka 2017a, pp. 32–33.

32 Listy polskie 1998, p. 428; Ragauskienė 2012, p. 40; Ragauskienė 2017, pp. 462–469.

33 Ragauskienė et al. 2015.

34 Elementa, XL, p. 31.

35 Ziembicki 1935; Kuchowicz 1989, p. 195; Kuklo 2009, p. 312.

not wished any offspring. Quite the opposite. It was expected that the unwelcome queen would not give birth to an unwanted successor even though at that time the dynasty in the male line was ending with Sigismund Augustus, and the young Jagiellonian monarch had not given any signs yet of being able to become a father. Barbara could not rely on the wishes that were heard by i.e. Queen Bona when she married Sigismund the Old in 1518. In his beautiful speech, the Primate of Poland and the Crown Chancellor, Jan Łaski (1456–1531), expressed a wish "of the entire country" to give the king only what he and his kingdom was lacking, i.e. a male heir.[36]

Barbara did not want to or could not meet the contradictory expectations of her husband, his family, courtiers, her own family, and finally, the nobility. The latter ones came to fruition on their own. Barbara Radziwiłł died childless, after being Sigismund Augustus' wife for only four years and a crowned queen for only half a year. After her death, the situation in Poland was similar to the one after the death of another beloved monarch's wife and unwanted queen on the Polish throne – Elizabeth Granowska (c. 1372–1420), the third wife of Władysław II Jagiełło (c. 1363–1434). When this Polish noblewoman, twice divorced and a mother of a few children before her marriage to the king, died in 1420, "this news – as written by Jan Długosz – filled the royal court and the entire Kingdom of Poland with great joy because they were all happy that their and the king's shame was erased." According to the chronicler, the king "showed sadness, but briefly".[37] Sigismund Augustus' sadness lasted much longer, and he cultivated the memory of his beloved wife until the rest of his life. Among the few expectations Barbara managed to meet in the short time she was the king's wife and the queen, was undoubtedly the one that the monarchs were rarely given – deep, passionate love that overcame obstacles and was ready for sacrifice. This one was enough to be remembered in Polish and Lithuanian history as one of the most famous and best known-queens.

Bibliography

Archive sources

BN [Biblioteka Narodowa = National Library], ms III.6614

---

36 AT, IV, p. 307; cf. Elementa, XXXVIII, pp. 102–105; Januszek-Sierdzka 2017, pp. 144–146; cf. Fleiner 2016; Woodacre 2015.

37 Długosz 1985, pp. 137.

Printed sources

AT, IV = Acta Tomiciana: epistole, legationes, responsa, actiones, res geste serenissimi Principis Sigismundi Primi, Regis Polonie et Magni Ducis Lithuanie, ed. Adam Tytus Działyński, vol. 4: A.D. 1516–1518, Posnaniae Poznań 1855

CDHung., IX, vol. 5 = Codex diplomaticus Hungariae eccesiasticus et civilis, ed. György Fejér, vol. 9, issue 5, Budapest 1834

Diariusz 1548 = Dyaryusz sejmu piotrkowskiego r. 1548, ed. Józef Szujski, in: "Dyaryusze sejmów koronnych 1548, 1553 i 1570 r.", ed. Józef Szujski, Cracow 1872 (Scriptores Rerum Polonicarum, vol. 1), pp. 161–297

Długosz 1985 = Jan Długosz, Roczniki czyli Kroniki Sławnego Królestwa Polskiego, vol. 11: 1415–1430, ed. Stanisław Gawęda, transl. Julia Mrukówna, Warsaw 1985

Elementa, XXXVIII = Elementa ad fontium editiones, vol. 38: Documenta ex Archivo Regiomontano ad Poloniam spectantia, VIII pars, H B A, B 2, 1548–49, ed. C. Lanckorońska, Rome 1976

Elementa, XL = Elementa ad fontium editiones, vol. 40: Documenta ex Archivo Regiomontano ad Poloniam spectantia, X pars, H B A, B 2, 1554–59, ed. C. Lanckorońska, Rome 1976

Elementa, XLIV = Elementa ad fontium editiones, vol. 44: Documenta ex Archivo Regiomontano ad Poloniam spectantia XIV pars H B A, B 2b, 1546–1567, ed. C. Lanckorońska, Rome 1978

Górnicki 2003 = Łukasz Górnicki, Dzieje w Koronie Polskiej, ed. Henryk Barycz, Wrocław 2003

Kutrzeba 1911 = Modus coronationis Barbarae Reginae Poloniae anno Domini 1550. Opis koronacyi królowej Barbary Radziwiłłównej z r. 1550, ed. Stanisław Kutrzeba, in: Stanisław Kutrzeba, Źródła polskiego ceremoniału koronacyjnego, "Przegląd Historyczny", 12, 1911, 3, pp. 305–307

Listy polskie 1998 = Listy polskie XVI wieku, ed. Kazimierz Rymut, vol. 1: Listy z lat 1525–1548 ze zbiorów Władysława Pociechy, Witolda Taszyckiego i Adama Turasiewicza, Cracow 1998

Listy polskie 2001 = Listy polskie XVI wieku, ed. Kazimierz Rymut, vol. 2: Listy z lat 1548–1550 ze zbiorów Władysława Pociechy, Witolda Taszyckiego i Adama Turasiewicza, Cracow 2001

Listy polskie 2004 = Listy polskie XVI wieku, ed. Kazimierz Rymut, vol. 3: Listy z lat 1550–1551 ze zbiorów Władysława Pociechy, Witolda Taszyckiego i Adama Turasiewicza, Cracow 2004

Orzechowski 1854 = Annales Stanislai Orichovii Okszii: secundum codicem Gymn. R. Thorunensis, ed. Adam Tytus Działyński, Poznań 1854

Modern sources

BEEM 2020 = Charles Beem, *Queenship in Early Modern Europe,* Red Globe Press, London 2020

BOGUCKA 2004 = Maria Bogucka, *Bona Sforza,* Ossolineum, Wrocław 2004

BRZEZIŃSKA 1999 = Anna Brzezińska, *Female control of dynastic politics in sixteenth-century Poland,* in: "...The Man of Many Devices Who Wandered Full Many Ways... Festschrift in Honor of János M. Bak", ed. Balázs Nagy, Marcell Sebők, Central European University Press, Budapest-New York 1999, pp. 187–194

COESTER 2011 = Christiane Coester, *Passages de frontières. Le voyage de le jeune mariée dans la haute noblesse des tempes modernes (XVe–XVIIIe),* "Genre & Histoire", IX, 2011, https://journals.openedition.org/genrehistoire/1469 (accessed on 28.11.2020)

DWORZACZEK 1974 = Włodzimierz Dworzaczek, *Maciejowski Samuel,* in: "Polski Słownik Biograficzny", ed. Emanuel Rostworowski, vol. 19, Wrocław 1974, pp. 64–69

FERENC 2006 = Marek Ferenc, *Królowa i jej brat. Stosunki Barbary Radziwiłłówny z Mikołajem „Rudym" Radziwiłłem,* in: "Faworyci i opozycjoniści. Król a elity polityczne w Rzeczypospolitej XV–XVIII wieku", ed. Mariusz Markiewicz, Ryszard Skowron, Zamek Królewski na Wawelu, Cracow 2006, pp. 149–166

FERENC 2008 = Marek Ferenc, *Mikołaj Radziwiłł „Rudy" (ok. 1515–1584). Działalność polityczna i wojskowa,* Towarzystwo Wydawnicze Historia Iagellonica, Cracow 2008

FERENC 2009 = Marek Ferenc, *Związki Radziwiłłów z dworem królewskim w 2. połowie XVI wieku,* "Barok", XVI, 2009, 2, s. 13–32

FERENC 2014 = Marek Ferenc, *Kobiety w życiu króla Zygmunta Augusta,* in: "Kobieta i władza w czasach dawnych", ed. Bożena Czwojdrak, Agata A. Kluczek, Wydawnictwo Uniwersytetu Śląskiego, Katowice 2014, pp. 301–323

FLEINER 2016 = Carey Fleiner, *Introduction,* in: "Virtuous or Villainess? The Image of the Royal Mother from the Early Medieval to the Early Modern Era", ed. Carey Fleiener, Elena Woodacre, Plagrave Macmillan, New York 2016 (Queenship and Power), pp. 1–8

VAN GENNEP 2019 = Arnold van Gennep, *The Rites of Passage,* transl. Monika B. Vizedom, Gabrielle L. Caffee, introd. David I. Kertzer, University of Chicago Press, Chicago 2019

GOŁĄBEK 2012 = Katarzyna Gołąbek, *Działalność publiczna biskupa włocławskiego Andrzeja Zebrzydowskiego w latach 1546–1551 w świetle jego korespondencji,* Instytut Historyczny UW. Wydawnictwo DiG, Warsaw 2012 (Fasciculi Historici Novi, vol. 12)

JANUSZEK-SIERADZKA 2010 = Agnieszka Januszek-Sieradzka, *Koszty uroczystości pogrzebowych królowej Barbary Radziwiłłówny,* "Roczniki Humanistyczne", 58, 2010, 2, pp. 29–55

JANUSZEK-SIERADZKA 2014 = Agnieszka Januszek-Sieradzka, De rege et uxore. *Kwestie małżeństw Zygmunta Augusta na sejmach,* in: "Manželství v pozdním středověku: rituály a obyčeje", ed. Paweł Kras, Martin Nodl, FILOSOFIA, Praha 2014 (Colloquia mediaevalia Pragensia, vol. 14), pp. 167–186

Januszek-Sieradzka 2017a = Agnieszka Januszek-Sieradzka, *Królowa Barbara Radziwiłłówna w dworskim mikroświecie*, Wydawnictwo KUL, Lublin 2017

Januszek-Sieradzka 2017b = Agnieszka Januszek-Sieradzka, *Oprawa liturgiczna koronacji królowych w Polsce w pierwszej połowie XVI stulecia w świetle* ordines coronandi *Barbary Zápolyi (1512) i Barbary Radziwiłłówny (1550)*, "Tabularium Historiae", 2, 2017, pp. 121–142

Kołodziejczyk 2015 = Anna Kołodziejczyk, *Barbara Radziwiłłówna – "niemoralna, nieczysta" królowa. Studium z obyczajowości staropolskiej*, in: "Czystość i brud. Higiena nowożytna (XV-XVIII w.), ed. Walentyna Korpalska, Wojciech Ślusarczyk, Collegium Medicum im. Ludwika Rydygiera. Dział Wydawnictw, Bydgoszcz 2015, 361–374

Kosior 2019 = Katarzyna Kosior, *Becoming a Queen in Early Modern Europe. East and West*, Palgrave Macmillan, Basingstoke 2019 (Queenship and Power)

Kuchowicz 1989 = Zbigniew Kuchowicz, *Barbara Radziwiłłówna*, Wydawnictwo Łódzkie, Łódź 1989

Kuklo 2009 = Cezary Kuklo, *Demografia Rzeczypospolitej przedrozbiorowej*, Wydawnictwo DiG, Warsaw 2009

Marchwińska 2001 = Agnieszka Marchwińska, *Początki dworu królewskiego Barbary Radziwiłłówny*, "Przegląd Bydgoski", XII, 2001, pp. 43–59

Marchwińska 2008 = Agnieszka Marchwińska, *Królewskie dwory żon Zygmunta Augusta. Organizacja i składy osobowe*, Wydawnictwo Naukowe Uniwersytetu Mikołaja Kopernika, Toruń 2008 (Roczniki Towarzystwa Naukowego w Toruniu, vol. 92, issue 1)

Marchwińska 2011 = Agnieszka Marchwińska, *Starania Zygmunta Augusta o uznanie Barbary Radziwiłłówny w Koronie*, in: "A Pomerania ad ultimas terras. Studia ofiarowane Barbarze Popielas-Szultce w sześćdziesiątą piątą rocznicę urodzin i czterdziestolecie pracy naukowej", ed. Jarosław Sochacki, Agnieszka Teterycz-Puzio, Wydawnictwo Naukowe Akademii Pomorskiej, Słupsk 2011, pp. 484–499

Mickūnaitė 2017 = Giedre Mickūnaitė, *United in blood, divided by faith: Elena Ivanovna and Aleksander Jagiellończyk*, in: "Frictions and Failures: Cultural Encounters in Crisis", ed. Almut Bues, Harrassowitz Verlag, Wiesbaden 2017, pp. 181–200

Mrówczyńska 1983 = Danuta Mrówczyńska, *Wzorzec społeczny królowej w Polsce w XVI wieku*, in: "Społeczeństwo staropolskie", vol. 3, ed. Andrzej Wyczański, PWN, Warsaw 1983, pp. 49–70

Muir 1997 = Edward Muir, *Ritual in Early Modern Europe*, Cambridge University Press, Cambridge 1997

Pastrnak 2020 = Patrik Pastrnak, *Bona Sforza's Bridal Journey to Poland as Imaginary Traveling and Jagiellonian Propaganda*, "Zeitschrift für Slavische Philologie", LXXVI, 2020, 2, pp. 289–315

Pociecha 1947 = Władysław Pociecha, *Arcybiskup gnieźnieński Mikołaj Dzierzgowski, prymas Polski (ok. 1490–1559). Zarys monograficzny*, "Nasza Przeszłość", II, 1947, pp. 37–102

Przybyszewski 1975 = Bolesław Przybyszewski, *Jadwiga i Wilhelm*, "Analecta Cracoviensia", VII, 1975, pp. 107–150

Ragauskienė 1999 = Raimonda Ragauskienė, *Barbora Radvilaitė*, Vaga, Vilnius 1999

Ragauskienė 2012 = Raimonda Ragauskienė, *Z historii biologicznej magnaterii Wielkiego Księstwa Litewskiego: linia Radziwiłłów na Birżach i Dubinkach w XVI w.*, in: "Sic erat in fatis. Studia i szkice historyczne dedykowane Profesorowi Bogdanowi Rokowi", vol. 2, ed. Elżbieta Kościk, Rościsław Żerelik, Piotr Badyna, Filip Wolański, Wydawnictwo Adam Marszałek, Toruń 2012, pp. 30–47

Ragauskienė 2017 = Raimonda Ragauskienė, *Mirties nugalėti nepavyko: Biržų ir Dubingių kunigaikščių Radvilų biologinė istorija (XV a. pabaiga - XVII a.)*, Lietuvos edukologijos universiteto leidykla, Vilnius 2017

Ragauskienė et al. 2015 = Raimonda Ragauskienė, Rūta Nadišauskienė, Daiva Vaitkienė, Laima Maleckienė, Dalia Regina Railaitė, Maleckas Almantas, Astra Vitauskienė, *Mitai ir klausimai apie karalienės Barboros Radvilaitės (apie 1522–1551 m.) sveikatą. Istorinės žinios*, "Lietuvos akešerija ir ginekologija", XVIII, 2015, 4, pp. 290–300

Rutkowska 2014 = Grażyna Rutkowska, *Status wdów po królach polskich z dynastii Jagiellonów*, in: "Kobieta i władza w czasach dawnych", ed. Bożena Czwojdrak, Agata A. Kluczek, Wydawnictwo Uniwersytetu Śląskiego, Katowice 2014, pp. 229–258

Sucheni-Grabowska 1996 = Anna Sucheni-Grabowska, *Zygmunt August król Polski i wielki książę litewski*, Wydawnictwo Krupski i S-ka, Warsaw 1996

Sypek 2009 = Karolina Sypek, *Pobyt w Polsce dam dworu Katarzyny Habsburg, trzeciej żony Zygmunta Augusta, w świetle Rachunków poselstw z 1553 roku*, "Kwartalnik Historii Kultury Materialnej", LVII, 2009, no. 2, pp. 171–182

Szujski 1886 = Józef Szujski, *Charakterystyka Zygmunta Augusta*, in: Józef Szujski, "Dzieła, seria II", vol. 6: *Opowiadania i roztrząsania*, vol. 2, Cracow 1886, pp. 115–131

Targosz 2007 = Karolina Targosz, *Królewskie uroczystości weselne w Krakowie i na Wawelu 1512–1605*, Zamek Królewski na Wawelu, Cracow 2007

Watanabe–O'kelly 2017 = Helen Watanabe-O'Kelly, *Predestined for conflict: The consort and her mother-in-law*, in: "Frictions and Failures: Cultural Encounters in Crisis", ed. Almut Bues, Harrassowitz Verlag, Wiesbaden 2017, pp. 25–36

Woodacre 2015 = Elena Woodacre, *Introduction*, in: "Royal Mothers and Their Ruling Children: Wielding Political Authority form Antiquity to the Early Modern Era", ed. Elena Woodacre, Carey Fleiner, Palgrave Macmillan, New York 2015 (Queenship and Power), pp. 1–9

Ziembicki 1935 = Ziembicki Witołd, *Barbara Radziwiłłówna w oświetleniu lekarskim*, in: "Pamiętnik VI Powszechnego Zjazdu Historyków Polskich w Wilnie, 17–20 września 1935 r.", vol. 1: *Referaty*, Polskie Towarzystwo Historyczne, Lwów 1935, pp. 144–162

Agnieszka Pawłowska-Kubik

Anna Jagiellon's Networks. Concerns for Maintaining the Family Position and the Jagiellonian Dynasty Heritage*

Abstract:

This article aims at analysing Anna Jagiellon's activities, which were undertaken in order to maintain the Jagiellonian family position and legacy. Anna's activity was manifested in activities aiming at the recovery of her mother's – Bona Sforza's – legacy, the execution of her brother's, Sigismund Augustus', and her sister's, Sophia's (Duchess of Brunswick), wills, the efforts to give the throne of the Polish-Lithuanian Commonwealth to her nephew Sigismund Vasa, and the care for favourable marriages for the family. In order to achieve these goals, Anna carried out a long diplomatic game. She sought allies among the most influential people of that time in the international arena. Surrounding them with the nets of diplomatic friendship, assuring them of her loyalty and respect, she did not cease to remember about obligations made to herself. Everything indicates that contrary to the general opinion, Anna had a certain political vision, which she consistently tried to pursue.

After Sigismund II Augustus' death in 1572, Anna Jagiellon (1523–1596), the daughter of King Sigismund I the Old and Bona Sforza, became the only living representative of the Jagiellonian Dynasty that ruled the Polish-Lithuanian Commonwealth since 1386, who was still living in the Polish-Lithuanian state.[1] Anna – previously remaining on the outskirts of the political life – played a significant role in the three subsequent interregna. In 1575 she was chosen the king of the Polish-Lithuanian Commonwealth by the nobility, and Stephen Báthory, Duke of Transylvanian, and one of the pretenders candidates to the throne, was chosen to be her husband. After his death, Anna Jagiellon forced through the candidature of her nephew, Sigismund Vasa.

---

* The article was written thanks to financial means from the following project "The Jagiellonian Era and Its Legacy in the 1st Polish-Lithuanian Commonwealth to 1795 – Political History, History of the Political System and Parliamentarism in the 14th–16th c." run by Prof. Krzysztof Mikulski, carried out by Polish Historical Association, financed by the Ministry of Science and Higher Education – "National Programme for the Development of the Humanities", no. 0471/NPRH5/H30/84/2017.

1 Her married sisters lived outside the country: Catherine, Queen of Sweden; Sophia, Duchess of Brunswick; half-sister from the first marriage of Sigismund the Old with Barbara Zápolya – Hedwig, Electress of Bradenburg.

Anna did not earn a good reputation in historiography. She was considered a woman without a political vision, and her image as being helpless in the face of events, carried by the course of history's statistics, was continuously created. Anna Jagiellon was denied cleverness and extensive open-mindedness. It was assumed that her only life's goal was to get married, and after Báthory's death – to have her nephew chosen as the king. Spinsterhood, weirdness, and bigotry were emphasised.[2] The aim of this article is to prove that in spite of popular opinion, Anna Jagiellon developed a certain political vision and consequently tried to pursue it. The article's main argument will focus on Anna's fight for her mother's – Bona Sforza's – inheritance and the efforts to execute the wills of Sigismund Augustus and Sophia Jagiellon, Duchess of Brunswick. Her activities in the field of arranging the family marriages and as a foundress will also be signaled.

Anna's first steps in political independence are linked with the death of her brother, Sigismund II Augustus (1572), and – perhaps even more so – with the death of her sister, Sophia Jagiellon (1575). It was the duchess of Brunswick-Wolfenbüttel that was Anna's mentor, who helped her navigate the intricate political issues. The execution of her mother's, her brother's, and her sister's wills would have made Anna one of the wealthiest figures in Europe. Sigismund II Augustus bequeathed to Anna, Catherine, and Sophia the entire moveable property and all land that belonged to the dynasty.[3] He also transferred the rights to inherit Bona Sforza's Italian properties and sums lent by Bona to Philip II (the so-called Neapolitan sums, 430 thousands of ducats, the annual interest of which was 43 thousands of ducats).[4] Importantly enough, after the sisters' death, the entire wealth was to become the property of the Polish-Lithuanian Commonwealth without being subjected to any further inheritance. In a codicil written down a month before her death, Sophia, Duchess of Brunswick, bequeathed her sisters half of the moveable and immovable properties, which she had received under the will of Sigismund II Augustus, and after Anna's death, Bona Sforza's inheritance was to go to Catherine's children (Sigismund and Anna). Sophia also bequeathed her sisters a significant part of the

---

2 Bartoszewicz 1882, pp. 206–207, 395–396; 400, 442, 495; Lepszy, Sobieski 1935, pp. 128–132; Jasienica 1975, pp. 14–15, 256–257; Wrede 1986, p. 16; Bogucka 2009a, pp. 88–89, 137–138, 180–187. Out of the above-mentioned works, only Julian Bartoszewicz tried to build a positive image of Anna Jagiellon.

3 Franaszek, Łaszczyńska, Nahlik 1975, passim.

4 After Bona Sforza's death, Sigismund Augustus began fighting for his mother's inheritance. He did not manage to execute the rights to the Duchies of Bari and Rosano. The king was granted the right only to the sum lent by Bona Sforza and interests rates of that sum, as well as to the jewels, silverware, and ornaments; Cynarski 1983, pp. 153–162; Polańska 2011, pp. 39–54.

wealth collected in Germany.[5] After her death, Anna was left all alone – without family's support, but with "advisors" ready to impose their will, and with numerous men willing to take over the Jagiellonian inheritance. Anna joined a fight in which it was necessary to have allies.

The senatorial and dignitary elites of the Polish-Lithuanian Commonwealth were reluctant to the execution of Sigismund II Augustus' will from the very beginning. The state's great financial needs and fear that huge properties would excessively strengthen the ruler's position meant that attempts were made to delay the execution of the king's will, and there were calls to even overturn the will. Initially, Anna took a determined stance, which was supported by Sophia, but this soon led to a conflict.[6] Seeing that she would not be able to push through her will, Anna was looking for allies. Her sister Sophia was an obvious supporter, but she did not decide to make a personal visit to the Polish-Lithuanian Commonwealth, which would probably have strengthened the undertone of claims by the two Jagiellonians. Therefore, Anna's focus naturally shifted to Sophia's "relatives-princes"[7]: Albert Frederick, Duke of Prussia, and John George, Elector of Brandenburg, who had been appointed by Sigismund Augustus as the executioners of his will. In her letters, Anna Jagiellon not only emphasised the ties between them but also mentioned the duties set out in the will, particularly in relation to John George, and entrusted herself to his care, reminding him of the execution of her brother's will.[8] However, the interest of the above-mentioned men in this issue was minimal. After the coronation of Henry Valois, Anna also asked the papal nuncio, Vincenzo Lauro, for intercession in the execution of her brother's will with the ruler.[9] Anna's inventiveness undoubtedly draws attention because even though the efforts to get Albert Frederick and John George involved in the fight for the Jagiellonian legacy were not successful, they should be recognised as a sign of initiative and an attempt to break the impasse, at which the princess found herself.

Ultimately, Anna renounced the rights to her brother's inheritance in accordance with the wish of the political elites of the Polish-Lithuanian Commonwealth, which was the condition for her coronation and marriage in 1576. Although she clearly

---

5 Capita codicillorum Illustrissimae Dominae Sophiae 24 Aprilis anno Domini 1575 confectorum excerpta ex polonicis per dominium Czarnicovium, NLA Wolfenbüttel, 1 Alt 23, no. 77, c. 154–162v and c. 163–170v (two copies); Pirożyński 1991, pp. 101–132.

6 Dubas-Urwanowicz 1995, pp. 143–151.

7 Anna Jagiellon to Sophia Jagiellon, Warsaw, 8 XII 1572, JP 1868, vol. IV, pp. 9–11.

8 Anna Jagiellon to John George, Warsaw, 7 III 1573, GStAPK, Rep. 9 Polen, 8a/b C, c. 77–78v; Anna Jagiellon to Albert Frederick, Warsaw, 21 VII 1573, GStAPK, Herzogliches Briefarchiv, B1, no. 327, no pages; Anna Jagiellon to John George, Cracow, 5 IV 1574, GStAPK, Rep. 6, no. 3, Fasz. 8, c. 102–103v.

9 Vincenzo Lauro to Tolomeo Gallio, Cracow, 8 V 1574, ANP 1994, pp. 205–210.

implied her dissatisfaction while signing the cession,[10] it should be emphasised that the final decisions were not unfavourable for her. Anna received a part of the Mazovian dowry insurance; she was granted eleven thousand zloty of income from the Lithuanian estates, 60 thousand zloty could be donated to courtiers and servants.[11] The queen was also given a lifelong permit for using the resources of the treasury in Tykocin.[12] In return for a rich payoff, Anna forfeited the inheritance, which she had little chance to access and which she would not be able to freely dispose of anyway. The transfer of material assets to the state's properties in Sigismund Augustus' will had already taken place earlier – during Anna Jagiellon's life – but also for an enormous compensation. This allowed Anna to strengthen her influence in Mazovia, maintain the position of one of the wealthiest people in the Polish-Lithuanian Commonwealth, and increase her authority through coronation.[13] It is worth mentioning that Anna Jagiellon made an effort to create a rhetoric of sacrifice and victimhood around the issue of cession, stating that she willingly intended to completely relinquish the inheritance for the benefit of the Polish-Lithuanian Commonwealth.[14] This proves the fact that Anna was consciously creating the image of a merciful ruler who was – first and foremost – guided by the wellbeing of the community and who was taking responsibility for the state's future. It should be noted that Anna Jagiellon knew how to change the plans of action and to decide to negotiate with the noblemen instead of being obstinately persistent, which could bring additional destabilisation of the situation in the country.

With their brother's death, Anna and her sisters also became the heirs of Bona Sforza's wealth. The interregnum in the Polish-Lithuanian Commonwealth and as many as three heirs, who did not always act together, created a favourable situation for the Spanish court to suspend the payment of interest rates or even to cease the payments altogether, not to mention the meeting of Jagiellonian sisters' claims to the Italian duchies. Anna quickly started a multi-fronted diplomatic activity. In November 1572, she sent the copy of Sigismund Augustus' will to Cardinal Stanisław Hozjusz. She asked for an urgent agreement regarding the legal records of Jerzy of Tyczyn and Stanisław Kłodziński.[15] Thus, Anna appealed to the experts on the

---

10 Orzelski 1856, pp. 224–225; Bogucka 2009a, pp. 137–138.

11 Stephen, the King of Poland, with the consent of the states gathered at the Sejm, provides his wife, Queen Anna, the rights to estates in the Duchy of Mazovia and the Grand Duchy of Lithuania, and determines the amount and conditions of this provision, Warsaw 6 III 1581, BCzart., ms 985 Perg., vol. IV/18; "Oprawa Krolowey Iej Miłości Anny" ("The Dowry Insurance of Her Grace Anna") Volumina Constitutionum 2005, p. 453; Bogucka 2009a, p. 146.

12 Borkowska 2012, p. 319.

13 Kosior 2018, p. 73. Significant income also allowed Anna for keeping a high standard of life at the court; Bogucka 2009b, pp. 101–102.

14 Orzelski 1856, pp. 222–223; Kosior 2018, p. 67.

15 Anna Jagiellon to Stanisław Hozjusz, Łomża, 28 XI 1572, JP 1868, vol. IV, p. 271–272.

matter and her brother's long-term associates who had experience in diplomacy and in the fight for Bona Sforza's inheritance. She outlined the plan of diplomatic actions in a letter to Sophia, informing that she had already turned for help to the pope and the French queen, Catherine de Medici; she had also decided that it was necessary to write to the King of Spain, Philip II, without delay.[16] While building the solutions favourable to her case, Anna Jagiellon did not forget about the kindness of the papal nuncio, Vincenzo dal Portico, as well as the papal legate, Giovanni Francesco Commendone.[17] She also asked the Vice-King of Naples, Antoine Perrenot de Granvelle, for support, thanking him for the favours showed by him in the past to Sigismund Augustus' interests in Italy and asking him for help in the future.[18] This letter deserves special attention as it is a testimony to Anna's attempts to build diplomatic contacts with a man who, in reality, was reluctant to Sigismund Augustus' claims, and he even managed to withhold the payment of interest rates. In the ongoing correspondence, Anna proved her rights to Bona Sforza's inheritance, but she knew how to outline the "black scenario" which could have been if the conflict had not been resolved. Asking the pope for supporting her claims, she simultaneously indicated that further misunderstandings could bring "a turmoil in Christianity".[19] In the following years, Anna Jagiellon still benefited from the favour and friendship of the pope and cardinals when negotiating the Bar affairs,[20] but she also made her husband, Stephen Báthory, involved in the activity.[21] She also did not forget about winning the emperor's support and kindness, asking for Rudolph II's help and support in a number of issues related to negotiating Bona Sforza's inheritance already in the 1590s.[22]

Anna was undoubtedly at the forefront of efforts and endeavours relating to her mother's inheritance. She was the one who carried out an extensive diplomatic action, to which she motivated her own sisters. Although not without a dose of scepticism, Sophia and Catherine decided to rely on Anna, authorising her to try

16 Anna Jagiellon to Sophia Jagiellon, Warsaw, 8 XII 1572, JP 1868, vol. IV, pp. 9–11.

17 Anna Jagiellon to Stanisław Hozjusz, Warsaw, 22 VIII 1573, BJ, ms 1136, c. 93–94v; Anna Jagiellon to Stanisław Hozjusz, Warsaw, 24 VIII 1573, JP 1868, vol. IV, pp. 279–280.

18 Anna Jagiellon to Antoine Perrenot de Granvelle, no place and date available, RS, Extranea Polen, vol. 128, no pages.

19 Anna Jagiellon to Gregory XIII, Warsaw, 26 XI 1574, ANP 1999, pp. 341–342. In the light of the known correspondence, George XIII seemed to support the solutions favourable to Anna Jagiellon; Tolomeo Gallio to Vincenzo Lauro, Rome, 18 XII 1574, ANP 1999, pp. 88–91.

20 Anna Jagiellon to Sixtus V, Warsaw, 3 VI 1589, Vetera Monumenta 1863, p. 102; Anna Jagiellon to Gregory XIV, Warsaw, 28 I 1591, Vetera Monumenta 1863, p. 194; Anna Jagiellon to Cardinal Paolo Emilio Sfondrati, Warsaw, 28 I 1591, Vetera Monumenta 1863, pp. 194–195.

21 Anna Jagiellon to Stephen Báthory, Cracow, 11 XI 1583, AN Cracow, Archiwum Dzikowskie Tarnowskich, ms 1232, pp. 37–40.

22 Anna Jagiellon to Rudolph II, Warsaw, 22 I 1591, HHStA, Polen I, 49, c. 87–88v.

to win back their mother's inheritance on their behalf.[23] It seems that Anna was much more familiar with the "Bar matters" than her sisters, and she understood the complexity of the Italian inheritance, which is confirmed by Sophia, Duchess of Brunswick, who stated that she did not understand the Italian matters and she could not discern them.[24] It is easy to guess that the claims of the Jagiellonian sisters were questioned in Naples in every possible way. Anna was required to prove that she was...Anna – the daughter of Bona Sforza and the sister of Sigismund Augustus.[25] Declarations of the inheritance were demanded, and the documents sent by her were refused.[26] Then the right to collect interest rates of the borrowed sums was granted only to Anna, and the cession made by Catherine and Sophia was subjected to analysis. The marriage to Báthory also brought unexpected complications. For it was deemed in Naples that Anna Jagiellon broke the existing friendship with the House of Austria through this step, which – in itself – was recognised as a pretext to withhold the payments.[27] Catherine Jagiellon wrote about it with indignation: "They want to oust the [...] Queen Her Majesty from everything, from rents and other cases, showing this way that Her Royal Highness is guilty of taking a Polish Christian, His Royal Highness, as her husband".[28] In the light of numerous problems with Bona Sforza's inheritance, with which Anna had to struggle, it should be regarded as a success that the interest rate payments from Naples were ultimately continued. On the one hand, it is due to the service of the queen's agents, and on the other – due to a great determination and will to fight that Anna Jagiellon showed. Consistent diplomatic activity, constant reminders of her own affairs, efforts to get support motivated by kinship and/or friendship produced results.

The death of Sophia, Duchess of Brunswick, on 28 May 1575 not only deprived Anna of her elder sister's support, whose authority Anna enjoyed, but also opened

---

23 Catherine and Sophia granted authority to Anna to fight for the Italian inheritance of Queen Bona Sforza; Anna's statement that Catherine, Queen of Sweden, authorised her to try to recover the Italian inheritance of Queen Bona Sforza that belonged to her, no place, 18 IX 1574, RS, Kungliga arkiv, Svenska drottningar under 1500-talet, ms K 73, no pages. Anna's statement that Sophia, Duchess of Brunswick, authorised her to try to recover the Italian inheritance of Queen Bona Sforza that belonged to her, Cracow, 20 V 1574, NLA Wolfenbüttel, 1 Alt 23, no. 55, c. 128–129v; published in: BUES 2018, pp. 123–126.

24 Sophia Jagiellon to Stanisław Czarnkowski, Schöningen, 9 VI 1573, JP 1868, vol. IV, pp. 72–75.

25 Stanisław Hozjusz to Anna Jagiellon, Rome, 6 III 1574, Starożytności Historyczne 1840, pp. 92–98.

26 Stanisław Hozjusz to Anna Jagiellon, Rome, 6 II 1574, Starożytności Historyczne 1840, pp. 90–92.

27 Stanisław Hozjusz to Anna Jagiellon, Rome, 11 II 1577, Starożytności Historyczne 1840, pp. 146–150.

28 Catherine Jagiellon to Stanisław Kłodziński, Stockholm, 6 X 1576, RS, Kungliga arkiv, Svenska drottningar under 1500-talet, ms K 73, no pages.

another battlefront – the duchess' inheritance. The fact that Sophia's stepson, Julius, could cause trouble had already been known in the Polish-Lithuanian Commonwealth for a long time. Despite Sophia's balanced and possibly conflict-free family politics,[29] the duchess did not manage to avoid an argument with Julius after her husband's death, and this reflected the vision of what could happen with Sophia's wealth after her death: "When she dies, the stepson will take everything from her".[30] After receiving information of her sister's death, Anna informed Julius about sending an envoy, the Crown's referendary, Stanisław Sędziwój Czarnkowski, who was to represent her at the funeral and carry out talks with the duke on her behalf.[31] Anna Jagiellon also turned to Julius' wife, Duchess Hedwig, requesting help, friendly reception and hearing the envoy out.[32] Hedwig was the daughter of Elector Joachim II Hector of Brandenburg and Hedwig Jagiellon – Anna's half-sister. By getting involved the "distaff-side Jagiellon" in this matter, Anna was most likely hoping for the duchess' support resulting from the ties of kinship and attachment to the Jagiellonian dynasty, which Hedwig liked to emphasize.[33] However, Julius acted in accordance with the worst predictions: he organized Sophia's funeral without waiting for envoys and he seized the entire inheritance.

The history of conflict over Sophia Jagiellon's inheritance was analyzed by Jan Pirożyński,[34] and thus, there is no point in repeating his studies here. However, it is worth paying attention to activities undertaken by Anna before appointing mediators and the imperial commission for examining the case of the inheritance, which will allow us to grasp the main directions of Anna Jagiellon's diplomatic action. The Swedish queen, Catherine, was the main ally in this conflict. Unfortunately, the Jagiellonian sisters often acted independently, and by formulating various entitlements, they provided an inducement to deny their claims. Stanisław Sędziwój Czarnkowski, who was sent to Duke Julius, was enjoying Anna's trust. He had been involved in the Brunswick affairs for a long time. However, the Crown's referendary was more interested in his own benefits, and while carrying out his own political game, he concealed some facts, acting to the detriment of his female principal.

---

29 More broadly on this in the context of Sophia's exemplary role as a stepmother: BUES 2019, pp. 669–694.

30 Catherine Jagiellon to Sophia Jagiellon, Stegeborg, 22 VIII 1572, JP 1868, vol. III, 267.

31 Anna Jagiellon to Duke Julius, Warsaw, 23 VI 1575, NLA Wolfenbüttel, 1 Alt 23, no. 73, c. 9–10v; Anna Jagiellon to Duke Julius, Warsaw, 25 VI 1575, NLA Wolfenbüttel, 1 Alt 23, no. 73, c. 25–25v.

32 Anna Jagiellon to Duchess Hedwig, Warsaw, 25 VI 1575, NLA Wolfenbüttel, 1 Alt 23, no. 73, c. 24–24v.

33 Hedwig to Anna Jagiellon, Wolfenbüttel, 4 X 1573, NLA Wolfenbüttel, 1 Alt 23, no. 53, c. 24–25v.

34 PIROŻYŃSKI 1993, pp. 65–90.

Anna Jagiellon did not limit her support only to Catherine and Czarnkowski, but – since she made it a habit – she decided to seek help also at the European royal courts. In autumn of 1575, she informed the referendary that she was going to seek the emperor's support, to whom Czarnkowski was to go without any delay.[35] Maximilian II did agree to support the claims of the Jagiellonian sisters. Nevertheless, even before the election Diet, he had asked Anna for supporting his son, Archduke Ernest, in the upcoming election of the king of the Polish-Lithuanian Commonwealth. In return, he had promised Anna some unspecified favours.[36] These unspecified "favours" could refer to the support of the Jagiellonians' claims in the fight for Sophia's inheritance. This put Anna in a very difficult situation that required the issue to be dealt with in a way that could let her still enjoy the friendship of the House of Austria, but without supporting the Habsburg's candidature. In a letter written to the emperor a few days after being elected the king of the Polish-Lithuanian Commonwealth, Anna did not mention this – after all – significant event, but she was putting herself under the emperor's protection as an orphan,[37] thus implying in some ways that what had happened had taken place without her consent. Anna once again decided to ask John George, Elector of Brandenburg, for help and to appeal for support in executing Sophia's inheritance that was her rightful part.[38] Anna once again undertook precautionary steps, trying to create a favourable atmosphere around her in order to resolve the conflict. Unfortunately, despite the support she received from many directions, Sophia's inheritance, which had been seized by Julius, was not returned.

It is worth noticing a certain characteristic trait in Anna's fight for the Jagiellonian legacy. Regardless of the assessment of the situation and the realistic chances for executing testamentary bequests, and the problems encountered throughout the fight, Anna was characterized by an incredible determination, will to fight, and decisiveness. She was getting involved in a conflict that had a chance for success with the same energy as in a struggle where – despite a considerable expenditure of time, commitment, and finances – nothing was achieved. This allows drawing conclusions not only on the queen's personality but also the matters of political vision, which – once shaped – was a benchmark and axis of Anna's activities for over twenty years.

In the context of Anna's fight for her mother's, sister's, and brother's inheritance, it is once again worth looking at her attitude in the times of interregna. Anna's lack of decisive support for any of the candidate during the second free election, so far

35 Anna Jagiellon to Stanisław Czarnkowski, Warsaw, 20 X 1575, RS, Sztokholm, Diplomatica Polonica, vol. 301, no pages.

36 Maximilian II to Anna Jagiellon, Prague, 29 VIII 1575, HHStA, Polen I, 26, c. 91–91v.

37 Anna Jagiellon to Maximilian II, Warsaw, 19 XII 1575, HHStA, Polen I, 27, c. 161–162v.

38 Anna Jagiellon to John George, Warsaw, 28 XII 1575, NLA Wolfenbüttel, 1 Alt 23, no. 61, c. 33–34v.

explained by her political indecision and lack of sophistication, could have had in fact a different background. Anna walked on fragile diplomatic ice – a definite support for the Habsburg candidature could take away her popularity which she started to enjoy among the nobility, while the support for other candidates could revoke the emperor's help in the execution of Sophia's and Bona Sforza's wills. In this context, refraining from openly supporting any of the candidates to the throne of the Polish-Lithuanian Commonwealth (at least until the moment when it was possible) seemed to be the wisest solution. The election of 1587 was a diplomatic challenge. Anna Jagiellon was openly supporting her nephew, Sigismund Vasa. However, the queen cared about good relations with the Habsburgs, who could be useful for her in the context of implementing her political plans. Therefore, even before the election Diet, Anna Jagiellon had stressed why she could not support the Habsburg candidature, simultaneously emphasizing the family ties linking the Jagiellonians and Habsburgs, and her kindness and friendship towards the House of Austria.[39] In the letters after the election, she drew attention to the legitimacy of Vasa's election and also to dangerous consequences that the Habsburg's intervention in the Polish-Lithuanian Commonwealth could cause.[40]

Anna's support for Vasa's candidature during the election of 1587 is usually understood as the queen's choice being dictated by blood ties, sentiment, and the willingness to transfer maternal feelings to her nephew. Undoubtedly, Anna treated Sigismund like a son, the feeling she expressed in her letters to him, but Anna's reasons for supporting Vasa's candidature should be rather considered more pragmatically. Only Sigismund, who was a descendant of the Jagiellonians from his mother's side, could successfully continue his efforts to recover Bona Sforza's and Sophia's inheritance, and his position in these negotiations was singularly strengthened by the crown of the Polish-Lithuania state. Therefore, Vasa was the only candidate who – by birth and due to obligations to his predecessors at the throne – had to fight for the Jagiellonian legacy. Although not free from sentiments, Anna's support was a sensible and deliberate tactic on the way to achieving the set goals. The transfer of rights to Sophia's inheritance to Sigismund III in 1592 was a confirmation of consistent politics pursued by Anna Jagiellon and the hopes that were vested in her nephew.[41] It is worth emphasizing that this way Anna fulfilled

39 Archduke Maximilian to Anna Jagiellon, Vienna, 17 VI 1587, BRacz., ms 27, c. 93; Anna Jagiellon to Archduke Ferdinand, Warsaw, 4 IV 1587, TLA, Ferdinandea karton 121 (I would like to express my sincere gratitude to Dr Aleksandra Barwicka-Makula for making this letter available).

40 Anna Jagiellon to Rudolph II, Warsaw, 25 VIII 1587, EaFE, vol. 15, pp. 176–177; Anna Jagiellon to Philip II, Warsaw, 25 VIII 1587, EaFE, vol. 15, pp. 181–182; Anna Jagiellon to Rudolph II, Warsaw, 28 VIII 1587, HHStA, Polen I, 39, c. 54–55v; Anna Jagiellon to Archduke Maximilian, Warsaw, 28 VIII 1587, BCzart., ms 2254, pp. 20–21.

41 Dogiel 1758, pp. 503–504.

one of the dynastic obligations, described in the sociological theory of dynasty by Wolfgang Weber – she not only handed over the financial and nonmaterial legacy but also developed the sense of duty in undertaking such actions in the future generations.[42]

Dynastic marriages, as an important part of foreign affairs, often bringing the strengthening of a family's position and the confirmation of old alliances (or the creation of new ones), were a subject of Anna Jagiellon's efforts in the context of Sigismund III's and Anna Vasa's relationships. First and foremost, it should be noticed that Anna not only gave her support at the stage of creating marriages, but she was also their initiator. Even before Sigismund Vasa's election to the throne of the Polish-Lithuania Commonwealth, Anna Jagiellon had proposed the marriage between Sigismund and the daughter of Charles II, Archduke of Austria, and Maria Anna of Bavaria – Archduchess Anne. However, the archducal couple had other plans towards their daughter at the time, as did the Swedish king, John III, who wanted to marry his son to Christina of Holstein.[43] The plans of both Charles II and John III were unsuccessful, and in this situation, the notion promoted by Anna Jagiellon was revisited. The marriage of Anne and Sigismund III finally took place on 31 May 1592.[44] On the one hand, building a permanent alliance with the Habsburgs through Sigismund's marriage or his sister's could have been motivated by the reference to the Jagiellonian marriages within the House of Austria and the willingness to pacify the country after the bifurcated election, but on the other hand – by the hope to successfully solve the conflicts over Sophia's and Bona Sforza's inheritance. Anna's associates openly admitted that this marriage could contribute to the recovery of the Italian estates.[45]

The marriage plans of the king's sister, Anna Vasa, were also of concern for Anna Jagiellon. Archduke Maximilian, Ernest, Matthias, or Andrew Báthory, Prince of Transylvania, were considered the candidates for the princess' hand.[46] Unfortunately, we do not know Anna Jagiellon's attitude towards the abovementioned candidates. According to the studies by Aleksandra Barwicka-Makula, Anna was supporting Anna Vasa's plans to marry Archduke Maximilian and even initiate the negotiations, which were conducted at the same time as the attempts to win the hand of Anne of Austria for Sigismund Vasa.[47] Bożena Fabiani assumed that Anna Jagiellon wanted to bring Anna Vasa to the Polish-Lithuanian Commonwealth and bring her up at her court in order to marry her off to a candidate for

---

42 Geevers, Marini 2016, pp. 10–11.

43 Barwicka-Makula 2019, p. 78.

44 On the wedding and coronation circumstances, see: GAŁUSZKA 2018, pp. 225–251.

45 Stanisław Reszka to Anna Jagiellon, Rome, [31 III] 1589, BJ, ms 159, c. 134v–135.

46 Ochmann-Staniszewska 2007, p. 125.

47 Barwicka-Makula 2019, p. 84.

the throne, and thus make her queen.[48] Even though it is difficult to find sources confirming this conjecture, it can be assumed that Anna – anticipating different scenarios of the developing events at the election – also considered a situation in which Sigismund Vasa would not become the king. However, it is certain that Anna Jagiellon strongly supported the plans for marriage between Anna Vasa and Margrave John George, the grandson of Elector of Brandenburg. Negotiations were carried out in 1594–1598.[49] Even a few months before her death, Anna Jagiellon was discussing this matter with Sigismund III, pressing for finalizing the treaties. Without hiding her joy, Anna announced her future work for the benefit of her niece's marriage, treating this matter almost as a crowning achievement of all the activities undertaken before: "For this will be the most sacred and the greatest thing in the world, and probably also the final consolation and joy for us".[50]

In order to complete the image of Anna Jagiellon as a ruler who was consciously creating the dynasty's politics, the founding activity of the queen should also be mentioned. Among her many initiatives, special attention should be given to the royal chapel in Wawel and the mausoleum of Bona Sforza in Bari. The royal chapel's condition and the level of religious practices were of constant concern to Anna. She also founded Sigismund Augustus' and her own tombs, which were to complement the family mausoleum and to exemplify attentiveness in commemorating the Jagiellonian dynasty, which was reaching its end.[51] For many years, Anna additionally donated vessels, robes, and liturgical vestments. As Agnieszka Januszek-Sieradzka pointed out, the care for the family mausoleum was motivated not only by religious reasons but also by a strong dynastic and royal duty as the last representative of the dynasty.[52] The mausoleum of Bona Sforza in the Basilica of St. Nicholas in Bari was undoubtedly a manifestation of Anna's dynastic politics. Placing the images of St. Stanisław (the most important patron saint in the times of the Jagiellonian dynasty, whose cult intertwined the national and dynastic notions) and St. Nicholas of Myra (patron saint of Bari) in the middle of the tomb was to indicate the relationship between the Polish-Lithuanian Commonwealth and Bona Sforza's hereditary. On the other hand, placing in the mausoleum the scene of the resurrection, the portrait of the founder, and of Sigismund III can be interpreted as an idea of the dynastic continuity or even the dynasty's revival.[53] The mausoleum in Bari was to remind

48 Fabiani 2014, p. 44.

49 Material regarding the talks are i.e. in: GStAPK, Brandenburg-Preußisches Hausarchiv, Rep. 32, V. 24.

50 Anna Jagiellon to Anna Vasa, Warsaw 16 VI 1596, AN Cracow, Archiwum Sanguszków, ms 67, p. 452.

51 Kowalczyk 1987, pp. 5–22.

52 Januszek-Sieradzka 2016, pp. 41–57.

53 Waźbiński 1979, pp. 59–87.

about the Jagiellonians' rights to the duchy and to indicate an heir in the fight for Bona Sforza's legacy after Anna's death. Both the royal chapel in Wawel and Bona Sforza's mausoleum in Bari were not only monuments to the Jagiellonian family pride but also the artworks of a specific political function.[54]

In the light of the discussed topic, there are no grounds to continuously treat Anna as a person who was passive and devoid of political vision. She was characterized by stubbornness and determination in implementing the planned tasks. Although not all of them ended in success, it was not due to Anna's passivity or mistakes, but because of circumstances beyond her control as well as the end of opportunities and influences not only of Anna Jagiellon, but also her associates, family members, or befriended rulers. Maria Bogucka, the author of Anna's biography, concluded that Anna was not Bona Sforza and was not intended to become one. She did not take after her mother's instinct for power, ingeniousness, or political inventiveness, but she was to be characterized by weakness, vanity, and lack of insight.[55] However, was this really the case? In the light of this examination, Anna – regarded as an odd prude, without ambition and political visions, as well as political skills, took upon herself a decisive fight for maintaining the dynastic position and the Jagiellonians' legacy, achieving some successes in this area, i.e. by recovering some of the Neapolitan money, introducing Sigismund Vasa to the throne of the Polish-Lithuanian Commonwealth, and arranging his marriage to Anne of Austria.

Bibliography

Handwritten Sources

AN Cracow = Archiwum Narodowe, Cracow:
Archiwum Dzikowskie Tarnowskich, ms 1232
Archiwum Sanguszków, ms 67
BCzart. = Biblioteka Książąt Czartoryskich Cracow (The Princes Czartoryski Library, Cracow):
ms 985 Perg., vol. IV/18
ms 2254
BJ = Biblioteka Jagiellońska Cracow, Cracow:
ms 159
ms 1136

54 Waźbiński 1979, p. 86.
55 Bogucka 2009a, pp. 88, 180.

BRacz. = Biblioteka Raczyńskich, Poznań:
ms 27
GStAPK = Geheimes Staatsarchiv Preußischer Kulturbesitz, Berlin:
Brandenburg-Preuβisches Hausarchiv, Rep. 32, V.24
Herzogliches Briefarchiv, B1, no. 327
Rep. 9 Polen, 8a/b C
Rep. 6, no. 3, Fasz. 8
HHStA = Haus-, Hof- und Staatsarchiv, Vienna:
Polen I, 26; 27; 39; 49
NLA Wolfenbüttel = Niedersächsisches Landesarchiv, Wolfenbüttel:
1 Alt 23, no. 53; no. 55; no. 61; no. 73; no. 77
RS = Riksarkivet Stockholm:
Diplomatica Polonica, vol. 301
Extranea Polen, vol. 128
Kungliga arkiv, Svenska drottningar under 1500-talet, ms K 73
TLA = Tiroler Landesarchiv, Innsbruck:
Ferdinandea karton 121

Printed Sources

ANP 1994 = *Acta Nuntiaturae Polonae*, vol. IX, vol. 1, ed. Mirosław Korolko and Henryk D. Wojtyska, Rzym 1994.

ANP 1999 = *Acta Nuntiaturae Polonae*, vol. IX, vol. 2, ed. Mirosław Korolko and Lucjan Olech, Rzym 1999.

Dogiel 1758 = *Codex diplomaticus Regni Poloniae et Magni Ducatus Lituaniae*, vol.1 part 1–2, ed. Maciej Dogiel, Wilno 1758.

EaFE, vol. 15 = *Elementa ad Fontium Editiones*, vol. XV, ed. Walerian Meysztowicz, Rzym 1966.

Franaszek, Łaszczyńska, Nahlik 1975 = *Testament Zygmunta Augusta*, coll. Antoni Franaszek, Olga Łaszczyńska and Stanisław Edward Nahlik, Cracow 1975.

Starożytności Historyczne 1840 = *Starożytności historyczne polskie*, ed. Ambroży Grabowski, vol. 2, Cracow 1840.

JP 1868 = *Jagiellonki polskie w XVI wieku*, vol. III, IV, ed. Aleksander Przezdziecki, Cracow 1868.

Orzelski 1856 = *Bezkrólewia ksiąg ośmioro*, vol. 3, ed. Włodzimierz Spasowicz, Petersburg Mohilew 1856.

Vetera Monumenta 1863 = *Vetera monumenta Poloniae et Lithuaniae*, vol. 3, ed. Augustyn Theiner, Rzym 1863.

Volumina Constitutionum 2005 = *Volumina Constitutionum*, vol. 2, part 1, prep. by Stanisław Grodziski, Irena Dwornicka and Wacław Uruszczak, Warsaw 2005.

Modern sources

Bartoszewicz 1882 = Julian Bartoszewicz, *Anna Jagiellonka*, Cracow 1882.

Barwicka-Makula 2019 = Aleksandra Barwicka-Makula, *Od wrogości do przyjaźni. Habsburgowie austriaccy wobec Polski w latach 1587–1592*, Katowice 2019.

Bogucka 2009a = Maria Bogucka, *Anna Jagiellonka*, Wrocław 2009.

Bogucka 2009b = Maria Bogucka, *The court of Anna Jagiellon: size, structure and functions*, "Acta Poloniae Historica", 99, 2009, pp. 91–105.

Borkowska 2012 = Urszula Borkowska, *Dynastia Jagiellonów w Polsce*, Warsaw 2012.

Bues 2018 = Almut Bues, *Zofia Jagiellonka, Herzogin von Braunschweig-Wolfenbüttel (1522–1575). Akten zu Heirat, Tod und Erbe*, Braunschweig 2018.

Bues 2019 = Almut Bues, *Dynasty as a Patchwork House, or the (Evil) Stepmother: The Example of Zofia Jagiellonka*, "Hungarian Historical Review", 8, 2019, 4, pp. 669–694.

Cynarski 1983 = Stanisław Cynarski, *Udział Stanisława Hozjusza w staraniach dworu polskiego o odzyskanie spadku po królowej Bonie*, "Studia Warmińskie", 20, 1983, pp. 153–162.

Dubas-Urwanowicz 1995 = Ewa Dubas-Urwanowicz, *Konflikt Anny Jagiellonki z dostojnikami litewskimi w pierwszym bezkrólewiu po śmierci Zygmunta Augusta*, in: "Z dziejów Europy Środkowo-Wschodniej. Księga pamiątkowa ofiarowana prof. dr. hab. Władysławowi A. Serczykowi w 60. rocznicę Jego urodzin", ed. Ewa Dubas-Urwanowicz, Antoni Mironowicz, Halina Parafianowicz, Białystok 1995, pp. 143–151.

Fabiani 2014 = Bożena Fabiani, *W kręgu Wazów. Ludzie i obyczaje*, Warsaw 2014.

Gałuszka 2018 = Justyna Gałuszka, *Jak Kraków witał arcyksiężniczkę? Uroczystości ślubne i koronacyjne Anny Habsburżanki i Zygmunta III Wazy w 1592 roku*, "Przegląd Nauk Historycznych", 17, 2018, 2 , pp. 225–251.

Geevers, Marini 2016 = Liesbeth Geevers, Mirella Marini, *Introduction. Aristocracy, Dynasty and Identity in Early Modern Europe, 1520–1700*, in: "Dynastic identity in early modern Europe: rulers, aristocrats and the formation of identities", ed. by Liesbeth Geevers and Mirella Marini, London New York, 2016, pp. 1–22.

Januszek Sieradzka 2016 = Agnieszka Januszek-Sieradzka, *Anna Jagiellonka jako fundatorka wyposażenia kaplicy Zygmuntowskiej*, "Teka Komisji Historycznej. Polska Akademia Nauk. Oddział w Lublinie", 13, 2016, pp. 41–57.

Jasienica 1975 = Paweł Jasienica, *Ostatnia z rodu*, Warsaw 1975.

Kosior 2018 = Katarzyna Kosior, *Anna Jagiellon: A Female Political Figure in the Early Modern Polish-Lithuanian Commonwealth*, in: "A Companion to Global Queenship", ed. Elena Woodacre, Amsterdam 2018, pp. 67–78.

Kowalczyk 1987 = Jerzy Kowalczyk, *Nagrobek królowej Anny Jagiellonki w kaplicy Zygmuntowskiej*, "Folia Historiae Artium", 23, 1987, pp. 5–22.

Lepszy, Sobieski 1935 = Kazimierz Lepszy, Wacław Sobieski, *Anna Jagiellonka*, in: *Polski Słownik Biograficzny*, vol. 1, Cracow 1935, pp. 128–132.

Ochmann-Staniszewska 2007 = Stefania Ochmann-Staniszewska, *Dynastia Wazów w Polsce*, Warsaw 2007.

Pirożyński 1991 = Jan Pirożyński, *Testament i kodycyl księżnej brunszwickiej Zofii Jagiellonki (1522–1575)*, "Biuletyn Biblioteki Jagiellońskiej", XLI, 1991, pp. 101–132.

Pirożyński 1993 = Jan Pirożyński, *Spór o spuściznę księżnej brunszwickiej Zofii Jagiellonki (1575–1672)*, "Biuletyn Biblioteki Jagiellońskiej", XLIII, 1993, pp. 65–90.

Polańska 2011 = Ewelina Lilia Polańska, *Sprawa barska i sumy neapolitańskie w zabiegach królewskiego dyplomaty Jerzego z Tyczyna w latach 1557–1572*, in: "Servitium et amicitia: studia z dziejów kariery i awansu w Polsce Jagiellonów", ed. Agnieszka Januszek-Sieradzka, Sandomierz 2011, pp. 39–54.

Waźbiński 1979 = Zygmunt Waźbiński, *Mauzoleum Bony Sforzy w Barii, przyczynek do dziejów polityki dynastycznej królowej Anny, ostatniej Jagiellonki*, "Folia Historiae Artium", 15, 1979, pp. 59–87.

Wrede 1986 = Marek Wrede, *Anna Jagiellonka: szkic biograficzny*, Warsaw 1986.

Aleksandra Barwicka-Makula

Queen Anne of Austria (1592–1598) in a Motherly Net*

Abstract:

The main characters of this article are Anne of Austria, Queen of Poland, the first wife of Sigismund III Vasa, and her mother, Archduchess Maria Anna of Bavaria, while the main topic is the relationship between the two women.

Maria Anna of Bavaria, who could excellently navigate the then European politics and complicated diplomatic relations, wrapped her daughter in a web of connections. She was the one who decided about the daughter's education and marriage, she surrounded her with people loyal to her (Ursula Meyerin, Georg Schiechel, and Sigismund Ernhofer), and at the same time, she was building up a net of correspondents among the Polish courtiers of the young queen and the members of the elites in power. While pursuing her own plans, she requested her daughter to take action to get the Polish-Lithuanian Commonwealth involved in the conflict between the Habsburgs and Turkey or to encourage her husband to carry out re-Catholisation activities in the Polish-Lithuanian state and in the Kingdom of Sweden.

The "motherly net" from the title also had a broader dynastic and court dimension. The relations between the Habsburgs and the Polish Vasas were not interrupted by Queen Anne's premature death. Through her efforts, Maria Anna of Bavaria led to the marriage between Sigismund III and Archduchess Constance, Anne's younger sister, which gave her an opportunity to further activities.

The first wife of Sigismund III Vasa was 19 years old when she got married. Her mother, Archduchess Maria Anna of Bavaria, was married at a similar age. The subsequent fortunes of both women were not analogous, though.[1] They were connected through the experience of motherhood and the support they offered their husbands in difficult relations with their subjects. They differed in political temperament. Maria Anna of Bavaria was not only interested in current politics, but she also wanted to have a real influence on it. For this reason, she created a network

* The article was written using materials prepared as part of the 2018/29/B/HS3/00907 project: Polish Courtier at the Royal Courts of the Jagiellons and Elective Kings: Rank, Value System, Role Model (Dworzanin polski na dworze Jagiellonów i królów elekcyjnych. Pozycja, system wartości, wzorzec osobowy), financed by the National Science Centre.

1 The most detailed biographic study on the first wife of Sigismund III Vasa was written by an Austrian historian, Walter Leitsch - Leitsch 2009 pp. 1144–1351. The author of the latest biography of Maria Anna of Bavaria is the German historian Katrin Keller – Keller 2012.

of correspondents of over 150 people who were scattered throughout the Habsburg countries and the most important European royal courts, which was a source of information but also a tool of political pressure.[2] Her husband's death weakened her position only temporarily.[3] She was not successful in satisfying her aspirations to take over the regency and rule in Inner Austria on behalf of her underage son Ferdinand. Contrary to testamentary bequest, she did not leave Graz and did not move to her dower lands. She contacted the imperial governor, Archduke Ernest, and convinced him to protect the interests of the widow and orphans. Tense relations between the members of the guardianship council – Emperor Rudolph II and Ferdinand, Archduke of Tyrol – developed her diplomatic skills. She knew how to appreciate dynastic ties and, therefore, she persistently sought favourable marriages for her children. On the other hand, Anne of Austria was content with a role of a quiet advisor to Sigismund III and an intermediary between her husband and her mother. She supported the king's politics. She showed no ambitions to create her own coterie or to consolidate the Austrian House's supporters in accordance with guidelines coming from Madrid, Vienna, or Prague. However, for nearly six years of her reign life in the Polish-Lithuanian Commonwealth, she was under her mother's great influence – surrounded by people chosen by the archduchess, she was in close contact with her through correspondence, listening to her letters' advice.

The "motherly net" from the title should be understood multi-dimensionally. Firstly, as a pressure put by mother on her daughter's education (selection of syllabus and teachers), and then on the choice of a husband for her. Secondly, as influencing the composition of the queen's court. Maria Anna of Bavaria made sure that the closest circles of the young sovereign consisted of people who enjoyed her trust and simultaneously played a role of the archduchess' informants on the relationships prevailing at the royal court and the situation in the Polish-Lithuanian Commonwealth. Thirdly, as undertaking activities limiting political independence of the young sovereign – Maria Anna of Bavaria assigned tasks to Queen Anne regarding foreign affairs, she called on her to undertake action to get the Polish-Lithuanian Commonwealth involved in the conflict between the Habsburgs and Turkey or to encourage the husband to undertake activities to re-Catholicise the Kingdom of Sweden. Fourthly, as placing an obligation to maintain ongoing contact through correspondence with the mother – Anne of Austria became obliged to send written reports once a week to Graz, to consult matters of grand politics as well as everyday life at court. The archduchess was her guide in the process of "becoming the queen".

---

2 Keller 2012, pp. 160–165.

3 Archduke Charles died on 10 July 1590.

The close relationship between the mother and daughter stemmed from the upbringing model adopted by the archduke and archduchess, which was largely borrowed from the court at Munich. Maria Anna of Bavaria – similarly to her mother, Anna of Austria[4] – supervised her daughters' upbringing and education.[5] Following the example of her own mother, she was bringing her children up in discipline and a spirit of religiousness. She selected appropriate courtiers and teachers for them. For a short time, she even considered educating her daughters in a female monastery in Leoben.[6] She paid great attention to needlework, even though she considered sewing and embroidering boring when she was young.[7] She wanted to prepare her daughters for the role of ladies of the court.[8] She brought out their love for art and music[9] and trained them in organising court's celebrations.[10] She demanded a lot, but she loved her children very much. She did not like to say goodbye to them, and thus, the children accompanied her on numerous travels.

Anne was growing up surrounded by the love of both parents. She lost her father at the age of 17 when serious talks were already underway on the matter of her marriage. Maria Anna of Bavaria set their tone almost from the beginning. She had her own preferences, to which she tried to persuade Archduke Charles. Initially, the Swedish candidate was not in the group of archduchess' favourites.

The project of marriage between the son of John III of Sweden and Archduchess Anne was born in the head of a Jesuit, Antonio Possevino, who started negotiations regarding this matter at the court of Graz towards the end of 1580.[11] However, the archducal couple was at that time more concerned with difficult relations with their Protestant subjects than the issue of marrying off their eldest – but still only eight-year-old – daughter. Perhaps a more prestigious candidate had been required already at that time. Four years later, Nuncio Giovanni Andrea Caligari supposed that Archduke Charles and Archduchess Maria Anna were hoping to marry Anne to Emperor Rudolph II.[12] Most likely, for this reason, the eldest daughter accompanied

---

4 Anna von Österreich (Archduchess Anna of Austria; 1528–1590) was the daughter of Emperor Ferdinand I and Anna Jagellonica (Anne of Bohemia and Hungary).

5 For more details, see: Keller 2012, pp. 15–18, Leitsch 2009, pp. 1147–1155.

6 She consulted her bother on this issue, and he advised against it. See: William V Wittelsbach to Maria Anna of Bavaria, Monachium, 5 IX 1589, Hurter 1850, pp. 511–512.

7 Keller 2012, p. 16.

8 A cookbook with 651 recipes was prepared for Archduchess Anne in 1589 – Weiss 2008, p. 123.

9 Koldau 2005, pp. 78–79.

10 Information on "carnival masks" was preserved in the sources – it was a costume spectacle with dancing prepared by Archduchess Anne and her ladies-in-waiting. Sebastian Westernacher to Archduke Ernest, Vienna, 8 III 1590, HHStA, Handschriftensammlungen W0083, ff. 610–617v.

11 Germanico Malaspina to Tolomeo Gallio, Graz, 5 XII 1580, NBGraz1, pp. 134–136. See also: Obirek 1997, pp. 100–107.

12 Giovanni Andrea Caligari to Girolamo Rusticucci, Graz, 3 VI 1585, NBGraz2, pp. 392–393.

them in their journey to Prague, where ceremonies related to awarding the Order of the Golden Fleece to the emperor and Archdukes Charles and Ernest were to take place. They were an excellent occasion to present the archduchess at the imperial court. However, twelve-year-old Anne did not make an expected impression on the thirty three years old Rudolph II.

In the autumn of 1585, the papal diplomacy resumed efforts at the court in Graz in order to return to the project of marriage between a Habsburg and a Vasa, and thus counter the plans of John III of Sweden, who at the time intended to marry his son off to a Lutheran, Princess Christina of Holstein.[13] The Swedish king's ambitions were also opposed by Anna Jagiellon, Queen of Poland, who – after the death of her sister Catherine (died 16 September 1583) – made efforts to ensure that her nephew remained a Catholic, which was to open up his way to the throne of the Polish-Lithuanian Commonwealth in the future. The sovereign got in touch with Antonio Possevino, who convinced her that Archduchess Anne would be the best candidate for being the wife of young Vasa.[14] However, a year passed before Anna Jagiellon decided to take the initiative in the matter of Prince Sigismund's marriage; perhaps she was held back by the fact she acted without consulting the court in Stockholm. In the spring of 1586, she sent a Jew, Mandel, to Graz.

The Polish queen's matrimonial proposition created a furore. It arrived at a wrong time since the archducal couple was at that time trying very hard to marry Anne off to Henry, Duke of Lorraine, the son of Charles III and Princess Claude of France. Maria Anna of Bavaria was a promoter of this marriage. The archduchess carried out talks on this matter through the court in Munich – her brother William V, Duke of Bavaria, and, in particular, his wife, Renata of Lorraine, the sister of Charles III.[15] Surprised with the arrival of Anna Jagiellon's envoy, she wrote to Munich immediately, asking for advice on how she should respond to the Polish queen's proposition. She also wanted to know the actual state of negotiations with the Duke of Lorraine. In response, the duke of Bavaria expressed his surprise at an informal nature of Anna Jagiellon's endeavours – acting through an envoy without an appropriate diplomatic rank and letter of credentials. Nevertheless, he advised to consult this marriage offer with Emperor Rudolph II and Ferdinand, Archduke of Tyrol, for he personally did not know much about the Swedish candidate. Contrary to the expectations of Maria Anna of Bavaria, he did not report on any progress in negotiations with Charles III, who refrained from making a binding declaration. However, knowing his sister's preferences, he promised to persuade his wife to once again send a messenger to Nancy in order to speed up the negotiations.[16]

13 Roth 1967, p. 21.

14 Antonio Posssevino to Germanico Malaspina, Warsaw, 27 II 1585, NB2/1, pp. 62–67.

15 More details in: Roth 1967, pp. 23–32.

16 William V Wittelsbach to Maria Anna of Bavaria, Munich, 17 VI 1586, Hurter 1851, pp. 481–483.

The archducal couple decided to refrain from giving an answer to the Polish queen until new information arrived from the Munich court. The preferences of Maria Anna of Bavaria and Charles, Archduke of Austria, did not change; they were still more in favour of a son-in-law from Lorraine than Sweden. However, they did not want to definitely reject the offer from the sovereign of the Polish-Lithuanian Commonwealth once and for all, they considered the possibility of giving their younger daughter, Maria Christina, as Sigismund's wife. They allowed the possibility of marriage between Anne and young Vasa only in the event of failure of the Lorraine marriage project.[17] On the advice of the Bavarian duke, Charles wrote to Prague and Innsbruck. Emperor Rudolph II responded positively to Anna Jagiellon's offer.[18] On the other hand, Ferdinand, Archduke of Tyrol, took a more reserved position. His concern stemmed from Prince Sigismund's faith – his position as a Catholic in a Lutheran country. He was worried whether the confession he professed would not interfere with taking over his father's inheritance, whether he would not be forced to convert. He advised discerning these matters better. Nevertheless, he did not discourage the marriage between the Habsburg and the Swede. He supported the idea of marrying off the younger archduchess to Prince Sigismund if the Lorraine project was happily finalised.[19]

Weeks passed, and Duke Charles III's answer, which would satisfy Maria Anna of Bavaria, did not arrive. According to the archduchess' mother, this answer was not to be expected since the French queen, Catherine de Medici, did not agree to the wedding of her grandson to the representative of the Austrian House.[20] The Swedish candidate was slowly getting the favour of Archduchess Anne's parents, in particular since his chances to win the Polish crown after the death of Stephen Báthory (who died 12 December 1586) became realistic.

The Habsburgs were ready to accept young Vasa at the throne of the Polish-Lithuanian Commonwealth, particularly if the representative of their house would sit at his side. Mutual relations were complicated only by a bifurcated election – from now on, Prince Sigismund was Archduke Maximilian's rival.[21] The court in Graz ceased the marriage negotiations waiting for further development of events. They were resumed after the treaty of Bytom and Będzin had been signed (9 March 1589) owing to the efforts of the Holy See, which assumed that creating the Habsburg-Vasa dynastic union was the best guarantee of friendly relations between the House of

---

17 Maria Anna of Bavaria to William V Wittelsbach, Graz, 1586, Hurter 1851, p. 483.

18 Roth 1967, p. 30.

19 Archduke Ferdinand to Archduke Charles, Innsbruck, 3 VIII 1586, Hurter 1851, pp. 484–487.

20 Roth 1967, p. 29.

21 Swedish Prince Sigismund Vasa was elected King of Poland on 19 VIII 1587; three days later, the emperor's brother Maximilian III of Austria (Habsburg) was appointed to the throne. The House of Austria's efforts to win the Polish crown were discussed in: Barwicka-Makula 2019.

Austria and the Polish-Lithuanian Commonwealth. It was approved by Rudolph II, Archdukes Ferdinand and Ernest, and William V, Duke of Bavaria. The court in Graz prepared the archduchesses' portraits, and the arrival of Sigismund III's deputation was awaited. The successful conclusion of negotiations was hindered by Archduke Maximilian's refusal to swear in the treaty of Bytom and Będzin, engendering a radical change in attitude in the Polish-Lithuanian Commonwealth towards the king's Austrian marriage, which made it considerably more difficult to undertake official efforts for the archduchess' hand. The Styrian court was also confused because of rumours about Sigismund III's negotiations with Ernest regarding the Polish throne succession and monarchical plans on returning to Sweden.[22] The archduke and archduchess were far more comfortable with the vision of their daughter's reign in the Polish-Lithuanian state than in distant, Lutheran Sweden.

The atmosphere of uncertainty and anticipation in Graz is well reflected in the letters of Maria Anna of Bavaria to her brother in February 1590. In the first letter, the archduchess complained about the lack of news from the Polish ruler,[23] despite assurances coming from Rome about a speedy arrival of the royal envoy who was to start making official efforts for the hand of Archduchess Anne on behalf of Sigismund. Simultaneously, she expressed doubts about the truthfulness of these reports. She also informed that she had received a letter from Prague from Wolf Rumpf, which included an explanation for reasons why Anne's portrait had not been sent to Poland so far – in fact, the imperial court took into consideration the possibility that after the meeting with his father in Reval (in the autumn of 1589), the king would not return to the Commonwealth. Since these assumptions were outdated, Rudolph II's advisor promised that the portrait would be dispatched soon. The archduchess was aware that Sigismund III still had to convince his senators to his matrimonial plans. According to her, among other serious candidates, apart from her own daughter, were also her niece, Maria Anna, Archduchess of Bavaria (born in 1574)[24] and Marie de Medici, Duchess of Tuscany (born in 1575), the daughter of the deceased Francesco I de Medici. In the opinion of Maria Anna of Bavaria, the decisive factor could have been the offered amount of dowry because the Poles liked money. In the second letter, she conjectured reasons for the Polish

22 Barwicka-Makula 2019, pp. 324–325, Leitsch 2009, pp. 775–779, 1157–1165.

23 Maria Anna of Bavaria to William V Wittelsbach, Graz, 12 II 1590, Stieve 1886, pp. 423–425.

24 The archduchess feared the competition from the Munich court, and she wanted to know the opinion of the Bavarian duke on this matter. She relied on his views so far, and she also counted on his help in the marriage negotiations and his support in the difficult task of completing the future queen's court. She was relieved to learn that William was happy about the "Swedish marriage" of Archduchess Anne. Cf. Maria Anna of Bavaria to William V Wittelsbach, Graz, 30 XI 1590, Stieve 1886, pp. 438–440.

court's silence on the question of marriage,[25] despite conscientious efforts of the papal diplomacy. Accoding to her, the reason for the silence was the opposition of a powerful chancellor, John Zamoyski, who dreamt of the crown, to the planned marriage between the king and the representative of the Habsburg family. She assumed that due to financial reasons, the Poles were considering the monarch's marriage to the duchess of Tuscany. The letters of Maria Anna of Bavaria – even though they are emotional in their nature, revealing hopes and fears related to her eldest daughter's marriage – prove that the archduchess was well-informed and aware of the Polish-Lithuanian state affairs and Sigismund III's situation.

Negotiations regarding the Habsburg-Vasa dynastic union were resumed only at the turn of 1590 and 1591 at the initiative of Rudolph II.[26] Encouraged by the imperial offer, Sigismund III sent Cardinal Jerzy Radziwiłł to Graz. The royal envoy arrived at the Styrian court on 18 March 1591.[27] Then he asked for the archduchess' hand on behalf of the sovereign of the Polish-Lithuanian Commonwealth. However, he did not specify which one of Charles II's daughters the king was making efforts to marry, which in turn greatly surprised their mother.[28] Taking into consideration their age, three – out of eight – living female descendants of the archducal couple could be taken into account: Anne (born in 1573), Maria Christina (born in 1574), and Catherine Renata (born in 1576). Maria Anna of Bavaria was also surprised with the proposed wedding date. Organising the wedding ceremonies for the autumn of 1591 seemed rather unrealistic to her, considering the time needed for finalising the matrimonial negotiations, preparation for celebrations, and arranging the court of the future queen. In a country where the nobility was in the vast majority Protestant, problems could occur with recruiting members of the archduchess' retinue. Thus, the foresightful mother immediately turned for help to her brother William, sister-in-law Renata, and sister Maximiliana in order to find a suitable chambermaid and ladies-in-waiting.[29] The cardinal's mission was successful.[30]

---

25 Maria Anna of Bavaria to William V Wittelsbach, Graz, 25 II 1590, Stieve 1886, pp. 425–426.

26 Secret instruction for Bishop of Wrocław Andreas Jerin and Baron von Schwartenau Richard Strein from 29 XI 1590, HHStA, Polen I 48, Polonica 1590 November, ff. 2–5, 6–9.

27 The archduchess expected Cardinal Radziwiłł's arrival since she had received the news that the Polish king wanted to negotiate the marriage terms. See: Maria Anna of Bavaria to William V Wittelsbach, Graz, 16 III 1591, Stieve 1886, pp. 455–458.

28 Maria Anna of Bavaria to William V Wittelsbach, Graz, 27 III 1591, Stieve 1886, pp. 458–460.

29 Ibidem.

30 Jerzy Radziwiłł left the city on the 26 or 27 March. He went to Rome in order to inform the pope about Sigismund III's positive attitude towards the Habsburgs and the royal plan of marrying the daughter of Charles II, Archduke of Austria; he was probably supposed to ask the Holy Father to support the monarch's marriage plans. The aftermath of Radziwiłł's visit to Graz was the cardinal's recruitment to the groups of archduchess' correspondents. Ten letters of Jerzy Radziwiłł to Maria Anna of Bavaria are preserved in the Vienna archives – HHStA, FK 44/26, ff. 1–34 v.

The second envoy of Sigismund III, Gustaf Brahe, arrived in Graz nearly at the same time as Jerzy Radziwiłł. The king entrusted the count of Visingsborg with a very delicate task – he was to assess the archduchesses' looks.[31] During his stay in Graz, Brahe secretly observed both archduchesses, Anne and Catherine Renata.[32] In order to see Maria Christina. who was growing up at the court of the Bavarian Wittelsbachs, he went to Munich. Perhaps the count also wanted to have a closer look at the daughter of William V, Duke of Bavaria – Maria Anna. He left Bavaria for Vienna, where he had a meeting with Sebastian Westernacher. During the talk with the imperial adviser, he was to confess that there was not a more beautiful candidate for the royal spouse than Archduchess Anne.[33]

After Sigismund III's envoys left, Maria Anna of Bavaria threw herself into the preparations. She commissioned a draft of the prenuptial agreement. She sent envoys to Prague, Innsbruck, and Munich in order to find out the current attitudes of the guardianship council members towards the planned marriage. She emphasised the necessity of obtaining answers from the Polish king to the following questions: does Sigismund III plan to return to Sweden in order to take over power there, or does he plan to stay in the Polish-Lithuanian Commonwealth? If he returns to his fatherland but does not accede to the throne, where will the royal couple live – together with his father or in a separate residence? How will the issues of setting and the future queen's court be regulated?[34] The archduchess made efforts for her daughter to have guaranteed freedom of worship (in case she will have to live in a Lutheran country) and a position compatible with her background. She made an effort for her daughter to become financially secured and received a guarantee of selecting courtiers. Keeping in mind the wellbeing of her child, she acted energetically and tirelessly, putting pressure on her guardians, recruited future supporters of the queen (Jerzy Radziwiił, Gustaf Brahe), simultaneously building her own network of contacts.

In the second half of June 1591, the guardianship council positively responded to Sigismund III's efforts to win the archduchess' hand; the only request was that the monarch should specify which daughter of Maria Anna of Bavaria he wanted to marry.[35] Rather unexpectedly, a new obstacle occurred in the negotiations – the

---

31 See: Jan Bojanowski to Krzysztof Radziwiłł, Warsaw, 13 III 1591, AGAD, AR V 1082, p. 191.

32 Leitsch 2009, p. 1176, Roth 1967, p. 56.

33 Brahe's words were cited by the proud Archduchess Maria Anna in a letter to her brother. Maria Anna of Bavaria to William V Wittelsbach, Graz, 27 V 1591, STIEVE 1886, p. 463. Gustaf Brahe, similarly to Jerzy Radziwiłł, joined the archduchess' correspondence circle. Three letters of the count to Maria Anna of Bavaria are preserved in the Vienna archives. See: HHStA, FK 43/14, ff. 43–48.

34 Leitsch 2009, p. 1177, Roth 1967, p. 61.

35 Rudolph II to Maria Anna of Bavaria, Prague, 13 VI 1591, HHStA, HaFa 24, ff. 85–88, Rudolph II to Maria Anna of Bavaria, Prague, 17 VI 1591, HHStA, FK 4, ff. 58–59.

eldest, Anne, was reluctant to marry without love, and she was afraid of living in distant Sweden.[36]

The Polish monarch's decision that his heart was more inclined towards archduchess Anne was reported to Maria Anna of Bavaria by Archduke Ernest.[37] The emperor's brother also informed about Sigismund III's plans. According to him, young Vasa – in the face of his reign in Sweden being threatened and the inability to keep both thrones – decided to return to the hereditary kingdom. However, he decided to assign the Polish throne to the archduke before his departure. Passing on this information served to prepare Anne better for the role of a consort of the heir to the Swedish throne.

At the beginning of July 1591, Maria Anna – together with the help of a trusted adviser, Vice-Chancellor Wolfgang Schranz, managed to break her eldest daughter's resistance.[38] On 19 August 1591, Sigismund III issued an official request for the hand of Archduchess Anne and announced that deputation would be sent in order to finalise the marriage negotiations in the person of Bishop of Kuyavia, Hieronim Rozrażewski, and Grand Marshal of Lithuania, Albrycht Radziwiłł.[39] The following months brought about a lively exchange of letters between the monarch, Maria Anna of Bavaria, and the emperor on the wedding date.[40] The archduchess kept postponing the date, making excuses about the enormity of preparations. Her attention was drawn to the issues of the bride price, settings, dowry, and the number of the archduchess' retinue.

The style of her actions is well reflected by a letter written to Wolf Rumpf in the autumn of 1591,[41] which is an expression of a "hunger for information" that consumed the archduchess. Impatient with the prolonging silence of the imperial adviser and her own informant, she kept asking him about progress in the marriage negotiations. She insisted that he acted in accordance with her guidelines. Maria Anna of Bavaria was absorbed by dynastic issues, activities for the benefit of maintaining the family's prestige. She knew the importance of representation and ceremonial. For this reason, she was concerned about the wedding date suggested by Sigismund III – she was worried there would be no time for preparing the ceremony and celebrations at a suitable level, for making necessary purchases,

---

36 Leitsch 2009, pp. 1177–1183.

37 Archduke Ernest to Maria Anna of Bavaria, Vienna, 1 VII 1591, HHStA, HaFa 24, ff. 94–101.

38 Dr Wolfgang Schranz prepared a special memorial where he listed and discussed reasons for which the archduchess should be married to Sigismund III. See: HHStA, HaFa Karton 24, ff. 104–109.

39 Sigismund III to Rudolph II, Cracow, 19 VIII 1591, HHStA, Polen I 49, Polonica 1591 August-Dezember, ff. 2–3.

40 It can be found in sets: HHStA, Polen I 49, Polonica 1591 August-Dezember and HHStA, HaFa 24. It was partly published in: HVHAI/1, pp. 256–258, 262–271.

41 Maria Anna of Bavaria to Wolf Rumpf, Graz, 28 X 1591, Hurter 1851, pp. 489–493.

for recruiting suitable retinue in terms of rank and numbers. She demanded that the Habsburgs contacted the Polish king regarding the number of courtiers who would be able to stay with Anne in her new homeland. She wanted to accompany her daughter on her journey to the Polish-Lithuanian Commonwealth since she wanted to get to know her future son-in-law and his closest circles better. She was displeased with the reports that the emperor was going to entrust the function of a wedding ceremony legate to Landgrave George Louis von Leuchtenberg,[42] who was to be accompanied by his spouse. The archduchess did not understand in what capacity the landgrave's wife was to join the journey. She did not want her to take care of her daughter as this opposed her own plans. Moreover, she demanded the landgrave was accompanied by a second imperial representative due to reasons of prestige. Maria Anna of Bavaria was a tough negotiator. Rudolph II accepted the fact that the archduchess would accompany her daughter on the way to the Polish-Lithuanian Commonwealth. He also chose Bishop of Wrocław, Andreas Jerin, as the second legate.[43]

The last stage of the marriage negotiations was initiated by the arrival of Sigismund III's envoys in Prague (13 March 1592).[44] The agreement regarding the dowry amount (45 thousand guldens), means of its payout, and provision was achieved only on 17 April.[45] Four days later, the royal emissaries left the imperial court and went to Vienna, where Archduchess Anne together with her mother, Maria Anna of Bavaria, had already awaited. The wedding *per procura* took place in the Augustinian church on the 3 May,[46] which was officiated by Cardinal Jerzy Radziwiłł, appointed *a latere* legate particularly for these ceremonies. A few days later, Anne of Austria left for her new homeland with the escort of over 800 people.

The first meeting of the newlyweds took place in the fields between Łobzów and Bronowice on the 26 May. The royal couple made a parade entry to Cracow on the same day. Then, on 31 May, the queen's coronation and marriage confirmation ceremonies were held. Worries expressed by Maria Anna of Bavaria that the wedding ceremonies would not have a suitable setting did not materialise. Celebrations took nearly two weeks – balls, artistic performances, tournaments, and lavish banquets

---

42 He was a deputy of margrave von Ansbach at the election Diet (*sejm elekcyjny*) in 1587. See: Leitsch 2009, pp. 1199–1200.

43 Instruction for the deputies was made by the imperial chancellery only on 30 April 1592. See: HHStA, Polen I 50, Polonica 1592 April-Mai, ff. 91–98, HHStA, HaFa Karton 25, ff. 246–251. In the end, the landgrave's wife was in Anne's retinue, but her presence was not particularly emphasised during the wedding ceremonies.

44 The course of negotiations was discussed by: Barwicka-Makula 2019, pp. 335–337, Leitsch 2009, pp. 1191–1202.

45 This was the date given to *pacta matrimonialia*. See: Dogiel 1758, pp. 272–275.

46 Leitsch 2009, pp. 1200–1203, Roth 1967, pp. 90–98.

were organised on the occasion of the royal wedding.[47] Polish celebrations were widely acknowledged in Europe, becoming the subject for as many as ten Italian, German, and Czech newspapers.[48]

The young queen quickly won the affection of courtiers and subjects, and she also won Sigismund III's heart. The Venetian deputy, Pietro Duodo, described her as a woman with a slim figure, nice face, pleasant, and polite. He assured that the king loved her very much even though only two weeks had passed since the wedding. According to the Venetian man, the monarch's feelings were reciprocated.[49] Maria Anna of Bavaria left the Polish-Lithuanian state calm about the future of her beloved daughter. She was happy with her son-in-law, who not only met her high expectations regarding the ceremony's organisation, but also won her over with his attentive manners. The royal couple accompanied Maria Anna of Bavaria all the way to the Polish-Silesian border – no tears were spared. Eyewitness and royal courtier, Jan Bojanowski, reported that the mother and daughter sat down for the farewell lunch with teary eyes, but the archduchess' sadness about her departure was greater, or she was less able to stop it.[50] Perhaps the awareness that they were parting forever prevailed for the time being[51] and the "letter conversations" would be the only form of contact.[52] However, she left her daughter in good hands, surrounded by a loving husband and people who had been carefully chosen for her and whom she trusted.

The closest circle of the young queen included Jesuit Sigismund Ernhofer as her confessor (previously he performed this duty at Charles II's court), Georg Schiechel as a chamberlain, and Ursula Meyerin as a lady-in-waiting. They were all obliged to send regular, weekly reports to Graz about the relationship at the royal court and the situation in the Polish-Lithuanian Commonwealth.[53] Ernhofer's unique position

---

47 More details in: Leitsch 2009, pp. 1207–1210, 1222–1245.

48 Zawadzki 1977, pp. 59–62.

49 Gintel 1971, p. 184.

50 Jan Bojanowski to Krzysztof Radziwiłł, Cracow, 22 June 1592, AGAD, AR V 1082, p. 215.

51 Maria Anna of Bavaria was given a chance to see her daughter once again in the late summer of 1595.

52 The Vienna collection of Haus-, Hof- und Staatsarchiv keeps 50 original letters of the Polish sovereign and 5 drafts of the archduchess HHStA, FK 40, ff. 1–271v., and HHStA, FK 47, ff. 1–12v. One of the queen's letters to her mother got lost in the cover for Sigismund III's letters with his mother-in-law HHStA, FK 41, ff. 27–31v. Only recently, we received access to a fragmentary edition that constitutes the main part of the master's thesis by Hanna Dobner, written at the University of Vienna in 2015. The author analysed 17 letters by Anne of Austria and 4 by Maria Anna of Bavaria from 1593–1594. The surviving letters are most likely 9–10% of the original number (the percentage can be doubled if we add the lost ones). See: Dobner 2015, pp. 11–21; Leitsch 2009, p. 6.

53 The collection of the Vienna Haus-, Hof- und Staatsarchiv preserves 18 letters of Sigismund Ernhofer (FK 42/28, ff. 39–139v), 20 letters of Ursula Meyerin (FK 44/8, ff. 1–91v.) and 42 letters of Georg Schiechel (FK 45/4, ff. 1–142v.). Works are currently carried out on editing Ursula Meyerin's correspondence as part of the project "Die polnischen Hofkorrespondenzen Ursula Mey-

was proved by intervention carried out by Maria Anna of Bavaria, at her daughter's request, with the General of the Jesuit Order, Claudio Aquaviva. The queen was concerned about the dismissal of her trusted confessor (and the archduchess – of her informant) as a result of denunciations from the Polish confreres who did not like Ernhofer's close relations with the royal couple.[54] The unique role of George Schiechel in maintaining a consistent contact between the Polish courts and the Styrian branch of Habsburgs also seems undeniable. He was not only the archduchess' informant, but was also sent a few times to Graz by Sigismund III in order to inform Maria Anna of Bavaria and archduke Ferdinand about important events in the Polish-Lithuanian Commonwealth. On the other hand, the courtly duties performed by Ursula Meyerin (*Kammerdienerin, Gesellschaftsdame*) did not reflect her actual position. She was Queen Anne's confidante and a right-hand woman, a person who enjoyed the king's trust. Her exceptional status was not changed even by Anne's death. Sigismund III entrusted her with the care of his offspring. After the king's second marriage, she became Queen Constance's guide; she introduced her to the secrets of the court and political life.

Ernhofer, Schiechel, and Meyerin were not the only informants of Maria Anna of Bavaria about the situation in the Polish-Lithuanian state. The archduchess' stay in the Polish-Lithuanian Commonwealth for nearly one month meant that the group of her correspondents was also joined by the king's confessor, Father Bernard Gołyński,[55] and the young queen's chancellor, Stanisław Fogelweder.[56] It has already been mentioned that Maria Anne of Bavaria exchanged letters with Cardinal Jerzy Radziwiłł and Gustaf Brahe. The information network also included the Crown's Vice-Chancellor Jan Tarnowski,[57] Marshall Anna Radziwiłłowa,[58] Piotr Tylicki,[59] chambermaid Barbara Warschenhauserin,[60] Ernhofer's successor – Fabian Quadrantinus, [61] and even John Zamoyski.[62]

---

ers. Deutschsprachige Netzwerke und Wissenszirkulation um 1600 zwischen Warschau, Graz und München", supervised by Dr Kolja Lichy in cooperation with Oliver Hegedüs (Justus-Liebig-Universität Gießen).

54 Cf. Dobner 2015, pp. 113–114, 167, 184. Eventually, Ernhofer left the Polish-Lithuanian Commonwealth due to his deteriorating health in March 1597. He died on 28 May 1597, soon after returning to Graz. Obirek 1996, pp. 6–10.

55 Three letters are preserved HHStA, FK 42/10, ff. 14–21.

56 Eleven letters are preserved. HHStA, FK 44/2, ff. 17–51v.

57 Only one letter was preserved. HHStA, FK 44/15, ff. 1–2v.

58 Only one letter was preserved. HHStA, FK 44/18, ff. 19–20v.

59 Only one letter was preserved. HHStA, FK 45/16, ff. 30–31v.

60 Two letters were preserved. HHStA, FK 44/28, ff. 5–10v.

61 Three letters were preserved. HHStA, FK 44/24, ff. 37–44v.

62 Three letters were preserved. HHStA, FK 47/8, c. 1–15v.

The archduchess' second visit to the Polish court (September 1595) was a chance to strengthen the relations. The almost four-week long stay is presented in the historiography mainly as a family meeting, which gave the opportunity to get to know the grandchildren – two-year-old Anne Maria (born on 23 May 1593) and three-month-old Władysław (born on 9 June 1595).

Walter Leitsch doubted whether the arrival of Maria Anna of Bavaria was political in nature.[63] However, it should be remembered that the archduchess visited the Polish-Lithuania Commonwealth on her way back from Transylvania where she had travelled to escort her daughter Maria Christina in order to give her as a wife to Sigismund Báthory, Prince of Transylvania. The relationship was a result of the political calculation of Rudolph II, who – in exchange for the archduchess' hand – demanded from Báthory to access the anti-Turkish league and to become militarily involved in the conflict between the Habsburgs and Turkey. The topic of struggles between the House of Austria and Turks was most assuredly discussed also at the royal court in Cracow, especially since Maria Anna of Bavaria had already sought help from Poland earlier.[64] An interesting aspect of the royal mother-in-law's presence was noticed by the chronicler, Reinhold Heidenstein, who reported that the opponents of John Zamoyski tried to turn her against the chancellor's politics and, by "stroking the cord of motherly love", they tried to use her influence over Sigismund III this way.[65] However, the archduchess' stay in the Polish-Lithuanian Commonwealth did not contribute to the development of negotiations regarding the accession of the Polis-Lithuanian state to the anti-Ottoman alliance.

The archduchess was more successful in building an effective system of communication and information exchange between Graz and the Polish-Lithuanian Commonwealth. Ties of correspondence were not interrupted even when the royal couple, Sigismund III and Anne, went to Sweden (August 1593 – September 1594). They lasted, despite concern about the letters' security and about keeping their contents secret – particularly after archduke Maximilian, pretender to the Polish throne, took over governorship in Inner Austria and ruled on behalf of the minor, Ferdinand of Styria (1593–1595). Maria Anna of Bavaria required from her correspondents to use cyphers and to use only trusted people as intermediaries. She requested her daughter to send copies of important documents. The Polish queen used additional communication channels – she often made notes in her letters that other people would write about a certain topic in more details (U. Meyerin, B. Warschenhauserin, G. Schiechel, S. Ernhofer). Matters for consulting included political issues (relations between Sigismund III and Charles IX and the House of

---

63 Leitsch 2009, pp. 1583–1588.

64 Maria Anna of Bavaria to Anne of Austria, [Graz] 5 XI 1594, Dobner 2015, pp. 198–199.

65 Heidestein 1857, p. 348.

Austria's representatives, difficult situation of Catholics in Sweden, war between the Habsburgs and Turkey) and dynastic issues (mainly matrimonial projects regarding Archduchesses Catherine Renata and Maria Christina). The preserved letters from the mother to her daughter prove that Anne was subordinate to her mother – she followed the motherly instructions, she answered her questions exhaustively, she often extensively explained her husband's "correspondence laziness".[66] Maria Anna of Bavaria was undoubtedly the young queen's guide around the secrets of political life.

The "motherly net" from the title also had a broader dynastic and courtly dimension. The successful endeavours of Maria Anna of Bavaria to marry her eldest daughter off to the Polish king resulted in creating a network of family relations – relations between the Polish Vasas and Habsburgs (Sigismund III's second marriage with his sister-in-law, Archduchess Constance,[67] marriage between Władysław IV with his cousin, Archduchess Cecilia Renata[68]), and the Wittelsbachs (Princess Anna Catherine Constance, the daughter of Sigismund III and Constance was married off to Philip William, Count Palatine of Neuburg, who was the son of Magdalene of Bavaria, the niece of Maria Anna of Bavaria).[69] Dynastic ties gave an impulse to creating channels of cultural exchange and political cooperation. Regular contacts between Graz and Cracow served for the flow of information – the archduchess passed on the news from Poland to the members of the House of Austria. Due to the transfer of information she built her position within the dynasty. Even the death of Queen Anne did not sever the network of contacts – Schiechel and Meyerin remained at the court in order to inform their principal about what was happening in the Polish-Lithuanian state and in the king's closest circles.

The political role of Maria Anna of Bavaria, her influence on the actions of Sigismund III and Anne of Austria are underestimated in historiography. A particularly interesting issue seems to be the archduchess' participation in secret negotiations of the king with Archduke Ernest regarding the transfer of the throne. Although her involvement in destroying the evidence of secret negotiations are noticed (burning of documents from Archduke Ernest and Sebastian Westernacher),[70] the role of

---

66 Moved only by the death of his daughter, Sigismund III added a few sentences to his wife's letter, sharing his sadness after over the loss of his child with his mother-in-law; from that moment, he started making this kind of annotations more frequently. Anne of Austria to Maria Anna of Bavaria, Stockholm, 26 VI 1594, DOBNER 2015, p. 162. Eighteen letters of Sigismund III to Maria Anna of Bavaria are preserved in the Vienna archives (HHStA, FK, Karton 41, ff. 9–52v.).

67 The daughter of Maria Anna of Bavaria and Charles II, Duke of Austria, born in 1588.

68 The granddaughter of Maria Anna of Bavaria, the daughter of Ferdinand II (Holy Roman Emperor from 1619) and Maria Anna of Bavaria (Wittelsbach), whose parents were William V, Duke of Bavaria and Renata of Lorraine.

69 More details in: Skowron 2019.

70 Leitsch 2009, pp. 1602–1604.

Maria Anna of Bavaria in Sigismund III's abandonment of his abdication plans remains silent. Did the archduchess persuade her son-in-law to remain in the Polish-Lithuanian Commonwealth, did young Vasa take into consideration her opinion on the matter? The marriage with Anne of Austria undoubtedly impacted the decision of breaking off the negotiations with Archduke Ernest. However, more research is needed to determine the actual role of Maria Anna of Bavaria in diplomatic contacts between Sigismund III and the Austrian Habsburgs in 1589–1592. In the later period, the archduchess' influence was significant, particularly her determination to pursue the wedding between the Polish king and her daughter Constance. The archduchess created a thread of understanding between the courts in Cracow and Munich, and laid foundations for the future relations between the Polish monarch and emperor Ferdinand II. Owing to her daughters, Anne and Constance, she contributed to rebuilding friendly relations between the Habsburgs and the Polish-Lithuanian Commonwealth.

Bibliography

Manuscript sources

AGAD = Archiwum Główne Akt Dawnych Dawnych, Warsaw, AR = Archiwum Radziwiłłów, V 1082

HHStA = Haus-, Hof- und Staatsarchiv, Vienna:
Handschriftensammlungen W0083,
Polen I 48, 49, 50
HaFa [= Hausarchiv Familienakten] 24, 25
FK [= Hausarchiv Famielienkorrespondenz A] 4, 40, 41, 42, 43, 44, 45, 47

Printed sources

Dogiel 1758 = *Codex Diplomaticus Regni Poloniae et Magni Ducatus Lithuaniae*, vol. I, ed. Maciej Dogiel, Wilno 1758.

Gintel 1971 = *Cudzoziemcy o Polsce. Relacje i opinie*, ed. Jan Gintel, vol. 1, Cracow 1971.

Heidestein 1857 = *Rajnolda Hejdensztejna sekretarza królewskiego, Dzieje Polski od śmierci Zygmunta Augusta do roku 1594*, vol. II, ed. Michał Gliszczyński, Petersburg 1857.

HVHAI/1 = The House of Vasa and The House of Austria. Correspondence from the Years 1587 to 1668. Part I The Times of Sigismund III, 1587–1632, vol. 1, ed. Ryszard Skowron et al., Katowice 2016.

NB2/1 = *Nuntiaturberichte aus Deutschland nebst ergänzenden Aktenstücken 1585(1584)–1590.* Zweite Abteilung: *Die Nuntiatur am Kaiserhofe.* Erste Hälfte:

Germanico Malaspina und Filippo Sega. (Giovanni Andrea Caligari in Graz), ed. Robert Reichenberger, Paderborn 1905.

NBGraz1 = *Nuntiaturberichte. Sonderreihe: Grazer Nuntiatur*, vol. 1, *Nuntiatur des Germanico Malaspina. Sendung des Antonio Possevino*, 1580–1582, ed. Johann Rainer, Vienna 1973.

NBGraz2 = *Nuntiaturberichte. Sonderreihe: Grazer Nuntiatur*, vol. 2, *Nuntiatur des Germanico Malaspina und des Giovanni Andrea Caligari 1582–1587*, ed. Johann Rainer, Vienna 1981.

Stieve 1886 = Felix Stieve, *Wittelsbacher Briefe aus den Jahren 1590 bis 1610*, vol. 1, „Abhandlungen der Historischen Classe der königlich bayerischen Akademie der Wissenschaften", 17, 1886, pp. 385–498.

Modern sources

Barwicka-Makula 2019 = Aleksandra Barwicka-Makula, *Od wrogości do przyjaźni. Habsburgowie austriaccy wobec Polski w latach 1587–1592*, Katowice 2019.

Codex Diplomaticus Regni Poloniae et Magni Ducatus Lithuaniae, vol. I,

Dobner 2015 = Hanna Dobner, *Briefwechsel zwischen Erzherzogin Maria von Innerösterreich und ihrer Tochter, Königin von Polen und Schweden, während ihres Aufenthaltes in Schweden 1593/1594 – Historische Analyse und Edition*, Vienna 2015, Universitäts Bibliothek Universität Vienna, https://othes.univie.ac.at/38905/, accessed: 1.02.2021

Hurter 1850 = Friedrich Hurter, *Geschichte Kaiser Ferdinands II. und seiner Eltern, bis zu dessen Krönung in Frankfurt*, vol. 2, Schaffhausen 1850.

Hurter 1851 = Friedrich Hurter, *Geschichte Kaiser Ferdinands II. und seiner Eltern, bis zu dessen Krönung in Frankfurt*, vol. 3, Schaffhausen 1851.

Keller 2012 = Katrin Keller, *Erzherzogin Maria von Innerösterreich (1551–1608). Zwischen Habsburg und Wittelsbach*, Vienna-Cologne-Weimar 2012.

Koldau 2005 = Lidia Maria Koldau, *Frauen-Musik-Kultur. Ein Handbuch zum deutschen Sprachgebiet der Frühen Neuzeit*, Böhlau Verlag Cologne-Weimar-Vienna 2005.

Leitsch 2009 = Walter Leitsch, *Das Leben am Hof König Sigismunds III. von Polen*, vol. I-IV, Vienna 2009.

Obirek 1997 = Stanisław Obirek, *Antonio Possevino SJ i jego misja do Szwecji*, „Nasza Przeszłość", 88, 1997, pp. 91–108.

Obirek 1996 = Stanisław Obirek, *Zygmunt Ernhofer SJ i jego relacje o polityce Polski z lat 1593–1596*, Cracow 1996.

Roth 1967 = Elke Roth, *Erzherzogin Anna von Innerösterreich, Königin von Polen und Schweden. Leben und Stellung in der habsburgischen Politik ihrer Zeit (1573–1598)*, Diss. Graz 1967.

Skowron 2019 = Ryszard Skowron, *Budowanie prestiżu królewskiego rodu. Związki rodziny Wazów z dynastiami europejskimi*, "Studia Europaea Gnesnensia", 2019, 20, pp. 55–81.

Weiss 2008 = Sabine Weiss, *Zur Herrschaft geboren. Kindheit und Jugend im Haus Habsburg von Kaiser Maximilian bis Kronprinz Rudolf*, Tyrolia – Verlag, Innsbruck Vienna 2008.

Zawadzki 1977 = Konrad Zawadzki, *Gazety ulotne polskie i Polski dotyczące XVI-XVIII wieku. Bibliografia*, vol. 1: 1514–1661, Wrocław 1977.

Damien Mallet

The Queen's Long Reach: Louise-Marie and France, 1661–1668

Abstract:
This article aims to present an overview of the correspondence network established by Pierre des Noyers in France on behalf of the Queen of Poland, Louise-Marie Gonzaga, between 1661 and 1668. Indeed, the archives in Paris and Chantilly show this network is not limited to official contact with high-profile noblemen like Condé. From the very beginning of her reign, the queen and her secretary cultivated a dense network of contacts at the court of France, people gravitating around the king or Condé, for instance.

Many of those contacts were from the Gonzaga family and their *obligés* or former ladies from Louise-Marie's court who went back to France. This article presents specifically the Mignot family. While this family initially benefits greatly from serving Louise-Marie Gonzaga in Poland, alliances with people at the service of the Prince of Condé and his son test the loyalty of its members: while the queen can reach any of them to contact Condé, their loyalty seem to shift in favour of the latter.

Between Warsaw and Paris, letters are handled by French officials or expatriates posing as middlemen. Archives reveal a complex network, carefully built to maximize security against any kind of espionage through the extensive use of deception and redundancy. This article includes a quick presentation of this infrastructure.

At last, this network is thoroughly tested between 1667 and 1668 with the death of Queen Louise-Marie and major policy changes in France regarding Poland due to the War of Devolution: the temporary withdrawal of French support to the Prince of Condé in favour of Neuburg. This period both shows how this network is dependent on conjecture changes but also how it can decisively influence decisions taken at the court of France.

Louise-Marie Gonzaga reached Warsaw after a long journey in winter 1646 to be crowned Queen of Poland[1]. For many observers, the arrival of a French noblewoman in Poland is the occasion for France to spread its influence in this

1 This journey is told in two different sources, one of which was published: Le Laboureur, 1647, and another unpublished record in AMAE, M&D, ms.1 and its copy Des Noyers 1821. Bely 2016–1 studies several other testimonies of the event.

kingdom[2]. Thanks to her secretary Pierre des Noyers, we know the queen kept many contacts in France[3]. Years later, the catastrophic Swedish invasion of 1655–1660 shows the queen's ability, still through her secretary, to mount propaganda and counter-propaganda operations in France aimed at smearing Sweden[4].

It is though, after the death of Cardinal Mazarin in 1661 that the queen's effort towards France starts to bear fruits. She advocated a deeper French participation in Poland as early as 1658, but this project was always rebuked by cardinal Mazarin. Starting in 1661, though, archives in Paris and Chantilly[5] show the beginning of a concerted effort to put on the Polish throne a French nobleman, first the Duke of Enghien, then the Prince of Condé himself. In 1665, the project reached full momentum. A new French ambassador in Poland, Pierre de Bonzi, is sent to lead this venture. It is only with Louise-Marie's death in 1667 that the pendulum swings back, and the Polish affair loses importance in Paris.

This effort is first and foremost diplomatic: it is through the correspondence of Pierre des Noyers with his contacts in France that one can see the extent of this cooperation between the Prince of Condé, the King of France and the royal couple in Warsaw. This network of correspondence is not limited to official contact with high-profile noblemen like Condé. From the very beginning of her reign, the queen and her secretary cultivated a dense network of contacts at the court of France, people gravitating around the king or Condé, for instance. Many of those contacts were from the Gonzaga family and their *obligés*, former ladies from Louise-Marie's court who went back to France and joined Condé's inner circle while sometimes, French officials or expatriates posed as middlemen. This is the network this article aims to present, from 1661 to 1668. Indeed, while Louise-Marie died in April 1667, the Election project, as well as her influence, persisted for several years through the dutiful work of Pierre des Noyers, the implication of the Condé family as well as the loyalty of many members of the pro-French faction.

Louise-Marie's entourage as a source of contacts in France: the example of the Mignot family

Among Pierre des Noyers' friends and contacts in France are persons from the queen's entourage. Louise-Marie is well known for the successful alliances she sealed for some of her ladies: Marie Casimire de la Grange d'Arquien married Great General and future King John Sobieski, Claire-Isabelle de Mailly married Great

2 See Serwański 2004, Serwański 2009.

3 See AMAE, M&D, ms 1.

4 Des Noyers 1859.

5 See BNF-BOULLIAU, AMCCh-R and AMCCh-P.

Chancellor Krzysztof Pac. What is less known is that women from the queen's entourage went back to France and kept serving her from Paris[6].

In Pierre des Noyers' *Mémoire du Voyage*[7], Madame des Essarts is a prominent figure among ladies at the queen's court. Her name is Claude Félicine Moulin. She's the daughter of Anne Gonzaga's treasurer Gabriel du Moulin[8] and married Charles-François Testart des Essarts, former councillor and *maître d'hôtel* of Louis XIV[9]. He is at first Louise-Marie's treasurer[10], then master of her wardrobe[11]. They leave Poland for France in 1650[12]. There, Madame des Essarts becomes responsible for the personal correspondence of the queen on the French side: she takes care of anything sent to Poland and dispatches mail coming from Warsaw[13]. She is notably absent from Chantilly's archives while being extensively mentioned or quoted in Pierre des Noyers' correspondence. She also partakes in the search for a new confessor for the queen with Anne Gonzaga and the Prince of Condé[14] as well as a new doctor in 1666[15]. Madame des Essarts appears as a cornerstone of Pierre des Noyers' network of correspondence, thus an important person for Louise-Marie since she can reach the Prince de Condé and his secretaries through her[16]. She dies in March 1667, which triggers a short dispute between her two nieces about who would inherit her role at the queen's service.

Elisabeth Chastrier, born Mignot, is the first. She is the spouse of Antoine Chastrier, secretary of the Prince of Condé[17] and a regular contact of the queen's secretary. She's a friend of des Noyers, and while she's mostly absent from the archives before 1666, much evidence hint at an earlier contact. Catherine Davisson, also *née* Mignot, is the second. She married Charles Davisson, son of William Davidson, astrologist and King John II Casimir's personal doctor, invited by Pierre des Noyers to Poland in 1651. He serves the Duke of Enghien[18]. After a tough negotiation where both appeal to the queen and her secretary, Catherine inherits Madame des Essarts' role while Elisabeth takes care of Pierre des Noyers' personal correspondence, which quickly becomes the main channel of communication between the pro-French

6 About the queen's court, see Fabiani 1976, Targosz 1975.
7 AMAE, M&D, ms 1.
8 Magne 1920, p. 36n.
9 Châtelet de Paris, AN, Y//194–197, Insinuations, f. 182v, 1658.
10 Grell 2013, p. 336.
11 Châtelet de Paris, AN, Y//209–212, Insinuations, f. 282, 1666.
12 AMAE, M&D, ms 1, p. 128.
13 Condé to Noyers, 31 X 1664, from Paris, AMCCh-R, t. VII, f. 362.
14 Condé to des Noyers, 18 VII 1664, from Paris, AMCCh-R, t. VII, f. 155.
15 M. du Puy to des Noyers, 11 VI 1666, from Paris, AMCCh-R, t. XI, f. 220 and next.
16 See below.
17 See below.
18 See below.

faction in Poland, Paris and Chantilly. Madame des Essarts also has a daughter, Charlotte Testart des Essarts, often named Madame de Garsanlan. Her husband Jacques also came to Poland with Louise-Marie and was Władysław IV's envoy to France to complain about the French Ambassador M. de Bréguy[19].

Condé's inner circle

Pierre des Noyers' second most important contact as the queen's secretary is none other than the King of France's cousin Louis II de Bourbon Condé[20]. As early as October 1660 and with Louis XIV's blessing, the Prince establishes contacts with Louise-Marie and her secretary[21].

Contacts are, of course, not limited to the prince or his son Henri-Jules de Bourbon-Condé, Duke of Enghien. Notwithstanding the fact letters are written by their secretaries, these secretaries are themselves contacts, some of them even good friends of Pierre des Noyers or relatives of the queen's entourage. First among them is Pierre Caillet, also known as Caillet de Theil ou Caillet-Denonville. He is a recurring contact in Pierre des Noyers' official correspondence. He is first *intendant du prince*, then one of his secretaries. In 1663, he is officially sent to Poland to seal the wedding of the duke of Enghien with Anne Henriette Gonzaga, the queen's niece[22]. This union is very important for the Polish nobility as, at the time, Enghien was a candidate for the throne. Caillet's very official mission hides another fact: he is an agent jointly sent by Condé and Mazarin to Poland to support the queen[23]. He stays in Warsaw from 1661 to 1662 but fails his mission: the Polish Diet twice rejected Louise-Marie's project despite wide support. Back from Poland, Caillet relays des Noyers' and the queen's letters to the court of France. He is then disgraced[24], which does not stop or even limit contacts between the two secretaries. Letters from Pierre Caillet includes reflections on the situation in Poland, news from France and the queen's and des Noyers' friends. Two other members of the Caillet family appear among Louise-Marie's contacts. François Caillet, always named 'the captain', is a

19 AMAE, M&D, ms.1, p. 156. M. de Bréguy has a terrible record of hiding information, keeping letters, and bad behaviour in the presence of Polish nobles, including one tasty story where he plays with the Primate's skullcap after having drunk too much alcohol.

20 See Beguin, 1999.

21 Condé to Noyers, 1 X 1660, from Paris, AMCCh-R, t. V, f. 64.

22 Farges 1888, p. 37–45. Caillet is described in the mission as "counsellor of the King [of France]".

23 Caillet is mentionned in Des Noyers to Condé, 20 IX 1661, from Warsaw, AMCCh- R, t. V, f. 238.

24 Caillet-Denouville to des Noyers, 4 III 1664, from Metz, AMCCh- R, t. VI, f. 415.

younger brother of Pierre Caillet who joins Poland's Foreign Army[25] until after the battle of Mątwy[26], when he decides to come back to France. His letters from Paris are quite similar to his brother's, but also mention French brother in arms he met in Poland: Guillaume de Pechpeyrou-Comminges, count of Guitaut[27], and M. de Brion[28] noblemen under the protection of the Prince of Condé. Jacques Caillet, often called Caillet de Chanlot, is Pierre Caillet's cousin, Condé's secretary during the Fronde and then his *intendant general de sa maison* from 1660 onwards[29]. Contacts between him and Pierre des Noyers are strictly professional, though very cordial.

Antoine Chastrier is another secretary of Louis II de Bourbon. He often writes letters on behalf of the prince and is responsible for mail ciphering and deciphering[30], but his correspondence also include personal letters sent to Pierre des Noyers. His wife is none other than Elisabeth Mignot, named Madame Chastrier in the archives[31]. Direct contacts between Antoine Chastrier and des Noyers start in 1664, with des Noyers back from France and Caillet in disgrace. After the death of Louise-Marie and Louis XIV decision to give his support to the Prince of Neubourg[32], Chastrier is removed from the scene. It is now Dominique de Chauveau who is in charge.

Dominique de Chauveau is, according to Katia Béguin, a person sent to Poland following the death of Louise-Marie mostly to recover money owed to the Duke of Enghien[33]. This debt amounts to around 100.000 *écus* and includes claims on some of the queen's belongings[34]. Chauveau does not react at all to any piece of information des Noyers writes about the situation in Poland; his mission is solely to solve this matter of debt.

---

25 Caillet le capitaine to des Noyers, 20 VIII 1665, from the camp near Costern, AMCCh-R, t. IX, f. 166.

26 Same to same, 3 IX 1666, from Dantzig, AMCCh-R, t. X, f. 360.

27 Comminges had to leave France "because of a duel where he was too successful". The Prince of Condé, the Duke of Enghien and Anne de Gonzague all pleaded with the queen to help him join the Polish army. Caillet Denouville to des Noyers, 28 XI 1664, from Paris, AMCCh-R, t. VII, f. 416.
The current state of research only knows one letter of courtesy from Comminges to Pierre des Noyers, 10 XI 1665, from Toruń, AMCCh-R, t. IX, f. 309. Also, see below.

28 Brion is also mentioned earlier as the man who sends to Poland letters from both Caillet le capitaine and Comminges' friends in France. Caillet le capitaine to des Noyers, 21 I 1667, from Paris, AMCCh-R, t. XI, f. 182.

29 Beguin 1999, p. 408.

30 Chastrier to des Noyers, 5 X 1669, from Chantilly, AMCCh-R, t. VII, f. 249.

31 See above.

32 See below.

33 Beguin 1999, p. 243.

34 "Pressures, theft, corruption, nothing was spared to wrest the booty from Poland", Beguin 1999, p. 281.

Life of a letter from writing to delivery

Thanks to the massive amount of letters sent by Pierre des Noyers on behalf of Queen Louise-Marie, we have good insights into the logistics involved in this correspondence. Of course, for safety reasons, the infrastructure is never mentioned to its full extent, but the corpus is large enough to give us some of its inner workings. The goal is simple in theory: gather information in Warsaw, send them to Paris and have the right letter delivered to the right person without foreign interference.

When the queen sits in Warsaw, the standard delivery delay is four weeks and uses *ordinaires*, which are regular post relays in Poland, northern Germany and France. In each major city, letters are handled by Pierre des Noyers' contacts or French officials. In Gdansk, these contacts include merchants and bankers such as M. Formont[35] or local officials such as Francesco de Gratta[36], master of the post and Pierre des Noyers' "friend and *obligé*"[37]. In Hamburg, Jacques Martin, former "consul for the French nation", is the preferred middle man[38]. Caillet Denonville also mentions several contacts in the United Provinces and in Brussels, but their names or professions are never mentioned[39]. Between Gdańsk and Hamburg, two ways are possible, should political difficulties arise. The first way is through Swedish-controlled Stettin, the second through Berlin in Brandenburg[40]. Pierre des Noyers mentions a third alternative through Breslau in imperial territory, which sounds quite unacceptable to him as it is almost certain letters would be opened and read.

When letters reach Paris, they are distributed according to their content. Madame des Essarts is in charge of the dispatch and relays letters to their proper recipient with one notable exception: between 1662 and 1663, any letter to the Prince of Condé goes through Caillet-Denonville first[41]. Financial matters are more often than not addressed to Pierre Formont in Paris[42], brother of M. Formont from Gdańsk and also a banker. The Prince of Condé and the Duke of Enghien have their own bankers, M. Benzon and Cortesia[43]. Merchants and bankers form a

35 Anna Gonzaga uses Formont as a middleman to write to her sister about her private affairs, while Condé and Louis XIV consider him as a trustworthy man. Caillet-Denonville to des Noyers, 16 I 1663, AMCCh-R, t. VI, f. 21 and 23. When Colbert sends money to Jan Hevelius after he lost his observatory in a fire in 1679, he does so through Formont: des Noyers to Boulliau, 17 V 1680, from Warsaw, ms 13021, f. 28.

36 About Francesco de Gratta, see Salamonik 2017.

37 Chauveau to des Noyers, 16 XI 1668, from Paris, AMCCh-R, t. XIII, f. 266.

38 Pelus-Kaplan 2016, p. 118.

39 Caillet-Denonville to des Noyers, 30 X 1662, from Hamburg, AMCCh-R, t. V, f. 392.

40 Des Noyers to Boulliau, 1 III 1680, from Warsaw, ms 13021, f. 2.

41 Caillet-Denonville to Noyers, 17 XI 1662, from Paris, AMCCh-R, t. V, f. 405.

42 De Langeron to des Noyers, 18 IX 1665, from Paris, AMCCh-R, t. IX, f. 222 and next.

43 M. Benzon and Cortesia to des Noyers, 1 III 1669, from Paris, AMCCh-R, t. XIII, f. 333.

large portion of des Noyers' contacts which further secures correspondence: it is quite easy to hide political content in the daily mass of commercial and financial information exchanged between cities[44]. There is a deliberate effort to hide this correspondence as much as possible and to maximize safe delivery and protection against any kind of espionage:

> I always send you a page with public news separate from the encrypted one, and in case our letters are stolen, to make sure there would be no apparent intelligence between us, I will always address it to *Madame des Essarts* to be forwarded to *Madame la Princesse Palatine*. This page will always be marked MD at the bottom, which means *Monsieur Denonville*, and I will write encrypted what can't be told otherwise.[45]

Pierre des Noyers' uses the dual correspondence, public and private, is nothing new at the time. He uses it already at the time of the Swedish Deluge and for the very same reasons. Madame des Essarts offers another advantage: an encrypted letter sent from Poland to her could always be about private matters from the Gonzaga family and do not rise as much suspicion as the same letter sent to one of Condé's secretaries.

There is also a secret way, also established by Caillet-Denonville, which passes through Amsterdam and, from there, uses express envoys instead of the regular post[46]. This implies the existence of additional contacts, as well as envoys whose mobility raise no suspicion, most certainly merchants. In the first apparent use of this two-way correspondence, the Prince of Condé uses the ordinary way to show a public posture and goes as far as looking unsure about who and how to greet and thank the Queen of Poland[47]. The same day, but using the secret way, the Prince is already collaborating with des Noyers on Polish matters[48].

Such a system is close to a full-fledge diplomatic correspondence[49]. Des Noyers' system extensively implements safety measures such as cyphering, multiple ways, use of merchants, deception, a false recipient and the separation between public and private letters. This system exists on top of any official correspondence between Paris and Warsaw, and its goal is to further Louise-Marie's agenda. As a political tool, this system of correspondence survives Louise-Marie and plays an important role in Polish politics at least until the election of Michał Korybut Wiśniowiecki.

---

44 Maurin 2016, p. 38.

45 Des Noyers to Caillet-Denonville, 15 XII 1662, from Leopol, AMCCh-R, t. V, f 433.

46 Ibidem.

47 Des Noyers to Caillet-Denonville, 1 X 1660, AMCCh-R, t.V, f. 64.

48 Condé to des Noyers, 1 X 1660, AMCCh-R, t. V, f. 63.

49 Bely 2016–2.

Conflicting loyalties among the queen's contacts

The Mignot family presented above is a perfect example of a group of person with dual loyalties. Their rise is almost exclusively due to the queen who took them to her court, which in turn gave them the opportunity to ally themselves with powerful families thanks to the personal relationship between Louise-Marie and Condé. Charles and Catherine Davisson have a particularly ambiguous attitude after the death of the queen: Charles serves the Duke of Enghien, but when Catherine writes Pierre des Noyers for his help and support, she calls him 'his protector' without any hesitation. They certainly hope for the continuation of Charles' pension the queen used to pay[50]. The dispute between Catherine and Elisabeth about who should inherit Madame des Essarts' position is not settled by some rational decision, but rather by comparison of their respective support. This is an obvious effect of conflicting loyalties, but whose consequences are rather limited since they are restricted to family affairs.

There is another occurrence of such dispute, with much higher stakes in June 1667. At the time, the Queen of Poland is dead but her legacy and political project very much alive, pursued by her secretary and her allies among the Polish nobility, the pro-French faction. A seemingly innocent event occurs in France at this time, the death of Madeleine de la Grange d'Arquien, heirless wife of the Guillaume de Pechpeyrou-Comminges, count of Guitaut who served in the Polish foreign army. As her name implies, she is from the same family as Marie Casimire d'Arquien, wife of John Sobieski. The count of Guitaut is a client of the Prince of Condé. Madeleine's death triggers a dispute over the castle of Epoisses in France. Condé, as the main executor, rules that the castle should be from now on the property of his client's family and no longer of the d'Arquien. This infuriates Marie Casimire d'Arquien, her father, John Sobieski[51], and puts the queen's party in an uncomfortable position: openly supporting Condé would certainly mean losing Sobieski family's support while supporting d'Arquien would certainly trigger retaliation from France or put an end to the whole election project. The queen is no longer alive and can't mediate. The situation escalates, Sobieski threatens to leave the pro-French faction[52], but the matter is settled with Marie Casimire d'Arquien's journey to France. The Prince of Condé, the King of France and the future Queen of Poland found a common ground[53]. The consequences could have been much direr.

---

50 2 000 french pounds according to Raczyński 1844, p. 371

51 Des Noyers to Condé, 10 VI 1667, from Warsaw, AMCCh-R, t. XII, f. 90 and its copy, AMCCh-P, t. XXXV, f. 358.

52 Des Noyers to Condé, 17 VI 1667, from Warsaw, AMCCh-R, t. XII, f. 91.

53 Poumarede 2016, p. 83. These demands are also mentioned in the diplomatic instructions sent to the Marquis de Béthune, FARGES 1888, p. 140–153

Raison d'État and the Sun King's almighty authority

As mentioned earlier, the death of Louise-Marie does not put an end to her political agenda. One of her major accomplishment is the establishment of a solid pro-French faction which survives her death despite its heterogeneity. Some nobles are interested in her political reforms, and some like the idea of the Prince of Condé as a King of Poland, while others support the King of France on the international scene and, as such, support Louis XIV's agenda in Poland. The cracks begin to show in this formation shortly after the death of Louise-Marie, not because she is no longer there to maintain any cohesion, but because of a shift of priority in France.

Spain is late in paying the dowry for Maria-Teresa, Queen of France and spouse of the Sun King. In 1667, Louis XIV chooses a forceful resolution to the situation by preparing for war, calling the Right of Devolution, an old custom from Brabant, as a justification. A war against Spain involves at least three front, one in North-Eastern France and the Low Countries with the Rhine River as a border. The King of France succeeds in neutralizing several bridges over the Rhine by striking a deal between local princes: they will not allow any army to cross these bridges. One of these princes, the Duke of Neuburg, is ambitious. Former husband of Catherine Vasa, a relative of King John II Casimir, he claims nothing more than the throne of Poland and wants France's backing in his bid. Louis XIV need those bridges shut and agrees, the election project is instantly put on hold[54], and Condé is sent to lead armies in this war. The Prince of Condé, as powerful as he is and as eager as he is to rise to the throne of Poland, must submissively agree to the situation. Pierre des Noyers, on behalf of the now-dead queen, can reach him through many ways, through many persons, but he can't do anything against the will of the king and the *Raison d'État*. Condé's loyalty is ultimately with his king and parent.

The new situation brings radical changes in des Noyers' correspondence: letters sent directly to the Prince and his son disappear from the archives. They were either destroyed on Condé's side or never written in the first place. The secretary's contacts at the time are M. Chastrier and, for some months, M. Chauveau. The reverse is also true; there is no longer any letter from Condé or Enghien to des Noyers.

The queen's long reach

The affair, though, is far from being over. Pierre des Noyers and most of the pro-French faction still support the Prince of Condé. According to the secretary and

54 Louis XIV to Béziers, 16 VII 1667, AMAE, Pologne, t. XXVII, f. 47

most of the pro-French nobles, Neuburg has no power base[55] and barely any support among the nobility[56]. Despite the official break in the correspondence between Warsaw and Chantilly, des Noyers keeps on informing the Prince through indirect means: the Condé circle mentioned earlier. With a lot of stubbornness and patience, the pro-French faction maintains its support for Condé and waits for another shift in the French foreign policy. The pro-French faction reasons that Louis XIV's support can only last the duration of the war or be the result of some kind of plot to increase Condé's chances by pulling him away from the attention of its adversaries[57].

Great Chancellor Krzysztof Pac, one of Condé's strongest supporter, has a plan: Louis XIV should openly support the lost cause that is Neuburg while sending the pro-French faction a secret message confirming that, should Condé be elected, he would agree to this choice and free Condé from any obligation at his court. To have him elected, the pro-French faction should split its support between other candidates, with some members adopting a neutral, detached and disgruntled position to exacerbate tensions at the Election Diet. When the whole assembly is in an uproar, and the situation looks inches away from spiralling out of control, one of them should put Condé forward as a reasonable compromise. This plan should be known in France, though there is no official channel available, and Pac's office as a Great Chancellor prohibits him from having direct personal correspondence with a foreign official or prince. Pierre des Noyers and his network established on the order of the queen are the solutions. He tells the secretary of this plan through his spouse Claire-Isabelle in April 1668[58], and this plan, in turn, reaches Chantilly in a letter sent to Chauveau and Chastrier. In October 1668, Ambassador Pierre de Bonsy is sent to Poland with a new set of secret instructions. The King of France agreed to Pac's plan, his policy shift in favour of Neuburg failed on the Polish side. At least, the bridges over the Rhine were secured, and his War of Devolution, successful.

What is more interesting though, is that already in June 1668, both Condé and Enghien answered positively to Pac's proposal, under strict conditions:

> If (…) this affair is already done and does not face any difficulty anymore, I can't see how the King would refuse, but if there is contestation, he'll support Neuburg (…). Please make sure that M. de Béziers doesn't discover anything about this [letter] which is for you alone, and take special care to whom you tell about it all because things are told and retold and there is no secrecy among most Poles (…). See if we can act, but do not write me anything about it".[59]

---

55 Des Noyers to Chauveau, 17 IX 1668, from Warsaw, AMCCh-R, t. XIII, f. 223.

56 Ibidem, f. 224.

57 Des Noyers to Chauveau, 29 IX 1668, from Warsaw, AMCCh-R, t. XIII, f. 235.

58 Des Noyers to Chastrier or Chauveau, 6 IV 1668, from Warsaw, AMCCh-R, t. XIII, f. 82.

59 Enghien to des Noyers, 18 V 1668, AMCCh-R, t. XIII, f. 126.

Patience and stubbornness bore their fruits. For the outside world, though, the situation remains the same. Des Noyers and Enghien even play a small theatre piece through their official correspondence, the second blaming the first for writing about the election: 'We are so far from thinking about this kingdom that, should every Pole offer us the crown, we would not take it.'[60]. Pierre des Noyers, of course, duly apologizes.

The election of 1668 did not go as planned. The pro-French faction fell into disarray, with Sobieski and Pac's rivalry tearing it apart, fuelled by other families and opponents to the queen. As surprising as it sounds though, Krzysztof Pac's plan worked extremely well. The Diet went violent, with each side vilipending the other. The nobility was bitterly split when Michał Wiśniowiecki was put forward as an alternative, ending the struggle in a few hours.

Conclusion: a fragile balance between influence and dependency

This short study showed the paradoxical nature of the queen's network of influence: it is a strong and powerful tool built on a rather unstable and fragile base, sensible to conjecture changes. The events of late 1668 show that Louise-Marie, even after her death, exerted a strong influence among the nobility and even French policy in Poland. Not only Neuburg's bid for the throne was a spectacular failure, but Louis XIV even had to revert to covert support for Condé or face the risk of losing all gains in the kingdom. Pierre des Noyers' network showed its strength by relaying information and plans to Condé even when all contacts between Chantilly and Warsaw were supposedly shut. Its extreme redundancy allows any kind of information to reach its recipient in due time by direct or indirect means and with a level of safety rivalling a regular diplomatic network.

On the other hand, this redundancy renders conflicts among the network's members inevitable, both in France and in Poland. There are also conflicts between family members, as shown in the Mignot family, with each member seeking the backing of one of their patrons. These frictions can cause a faction to split if they appear among prominent people: John Sobieski threatened to move away from the Election project because of the Guitaut affair.

At last, the queen's network is only as powerful as she is, this is demonstrated by the French posture about Neuburg and Condé. The pro-French faction pushes Louis XIV to support Condé again in 1668, but is most likely because the King saw reasonable chances of success in Pierre des Noyers' reports and analysis. It was done because it was the right move for French interests: with the War of Devolution

60 Enghien to des Noyers, 23 III 1668, AMCCh-R, t. XII, f. 74.

over, the bridges over the Rhine are no longer critical and, while Louis XIV insists on keeping his word and supports Neuburg publicly, the opportunity to see Condé become King of Poland is too good to pass. The queen's network did not directly provoke the policy change but still provided the opportunity for its implementation.

Bibliography

Manuscript sources

AMAE [Archives du Ministère des Affaires Etrangères] M&D, ms.1 = Pierre des Noyers, Mémoire du Voyage de Madame Louise-Marie de Gonzague de Clèves, pour aller prendre possession de la Couronne de Pologne, et quelques remarques des choses qui luy sont arrivées dans le pays, AMAE, ms 1, Mémoire et documents, La Courneuve. See also Des Noyers 1821

AMCCh-P [Archives du Musée Condé à Chantilly] Chantilly, Série P, t. 24, 27, 29, 33, 35, 36, 37 and 38

AMCCh-R [Archives du Musée Condé à Chantilly] Chantilly, Série R, t. I-XVI (1645–1673)

Des Noyers 1821 = Des Noyers, Pierre, Mémoire du Voyage de Madame Louise-Marie de Gonzague de Clèves, pour aller prendre possession de la Couronne de Pologne, et quelques remarques des choses qui luy sont arrivées dans le pays, BCZ, ms 1970 IV, copy of AMAE, M&D, ms 1.

BNF-BOULLIAU = Correspondance et papiers politiques et astronomiques d'Ismaël Boulliau (1605–1694). I-V Lettres de Desnoyers, secrétaire des commandements de la reine de Pologne, Marie de Gonzague, écrites la plupart de Varsovie à Boulliau (1655–1692). BNF [Bibliothèque Nationale de France] Département des manuscrits, Français, ms 13019–3023

Printed sources

Des Noyers 1859 = Pierre des Noyers, Lettres de Pierre des Noyers, secrétaire de la reine de Pologne Marie-Louise de Gonzague, princesse de Mantoue et de Nevers, pour servir à l'histoire de la Pologne et de la Suède de 1655 à 1659, B. Behr, Berlin 1859.

Le Laboureur 1647 = Jean Le Laboureur, Relation du voyage de la Royne de Pologne et du retour de la Madame Maréchale de Guébriant, ambassadrice extraordinaire et surintendante de sa conduite, Jean Camysat et Pierre Le Petit, Paris 1647.

Farges 1888 = Louis Farges, Recueil des instructions données aux ambassadeurs et ministres de France: depuis les traités de Westphalie jusqu'à la Révolution française. Pologne, tome premier, Ancienne librairie Germer Baillère et cie, Felix Alcan, Paris 1888.

Magne 1920 = Émil Magne, Lettres inédites à Marie-Louise de Gonzague, reine de Pologne, sur la cour de Louis XIV (1660–1667), Emile-Paul Frères, Paris 1920.

Raczyński 1844 = Edward Raczyński, Portfolio królowej Maryi Ludwiki, t. I-II, w drukarni i księgarni Nowej, Poznań 1844.

Modern sources

Beguin 1999 = Beguin, Katia, *Les princes de Condés. Rebelles, courtisans et mécènes dans la France du Grand Siècle*, Champ Vallon, Seyssel 1999.

Bely 2016a = Lucien Bély, *Un mariage, un voyage, des témoignages*, in: France-Pologne, contacts, échanges, culturels, représentations, Honoré Champion, Paris 2016.

Bely 2016b, Lucien Bély, *La surveillance des courriers. Une dimension de l'action diplomatique*, in: La Poste, servante et actrice des relations internationales (XVIe-XIXe), Brussels, 2016.

Fabiani 1976 = Bożena Fabiani, *Warszawski dwór Ludwiki Marii*, Państwowy Instytut Wydawniczy, Warsaw 1976.

Grell 2013 = Chantal Grell, *Pierre des Noyers ou les curiosités d'un savant diplomate*, in: L'Homme au risque de l'infini: mélange d'histoire et de philosophie des sciences offerts à Michel Blay, Brepols, Turnhout 2013.

Maurin 2016 = Olivier Maurin, *Transmettre les correspondances du baron de Wettes et du marquis des Alleurs au-delà du Saint-Empire. Le réseau postal européen de la diplomatie française*, in: La Poste, servante et actrice des relations internationales (XVIe-XIXe), Brussels, 2016.

Pelus-Kaplan 2016 =, Marie-Louise Pelus-Kaplan, *Un consul français à Gdańsk: quel intérêt pour les relations franco-polonaises?*, in: France-Pologne, contacts, échanges, culturels, représentations, Honoré Champion, Paris 2016.

Poumarede 2016 = Géraud Poumarède, *"Fidèle sujette" ou "Mauvaise française" ? Marie-Casimire de la Grange d'Arquien reine de Pologne, sous le regard des ambassadeurs de Louis XIV*, in: France-Pologne, contacts, échanges, culturels, représentations, Honoré Champion, Paris 2016.

Salamonik 2017 = Michał Salamonik, *In Their Majesties' Service: The Career of Francesco De Gratta (1613–1676) as a Royal Servant and Trader in Gdańsk*, Huddinge: Södertörns högskola, 2017.

Serwański 2004 = Maciej Serwański, *La Pologne dans la rivalité entre la maison d'Autriche et la France (XVIe-XVIIIe siècles), essai de synthèse*, in: La Pologne et l'Europe occidentale du Moyen-Age à nos jours: Actes du colloque organisé par l'Université Paris VII-Denis Diderot, Paris, les 28 et 29 octobre 1999, Instytut Historii UAM, Paris-Poznań 2004.

Serwański 20049= Maciej Serwański, *Missions diplomatiques françaises en Pologne au XVIIe siècle*, in: Le rayonnement français en Europe centrale du XVIIe siècle à nos jours, Maison des Sciences de l'Homme d'Aquitaine, Pessac 2009.

Targosz 1975 = Karolina Targosz, *Uczony dwór Ludwiki Marii Gonzagi (1646–1667)*, Ossolineum, Cracow 1975.

Dominika Rychel-Mantur

Queen Marie Casimire Forming a Network of Affinities – an Attempt to Pursue Dynastic Politics*

Abstract:

After a few years of affair and the death of her husband, Marie Casimire de la Grange d'Arquien married the Grand Marshall of the Crown, John Sobieski, in order to take the Polish throne by his side. Just after the election, the position of the new ruler's wife triggered the dissatisfaction of his previous political enemies. Attempts were made to refuse her the position of the queen and then to not let the coronation take place, which John III prevented. Standing unshakeably by her husband's side and promoting her offspring – particularly the sons who could follow in the footsteps of their father and ascend the throne – Marie Casimire spared no effort to secure her family's future. Therefore, she tried to build a network of connections and influences which were to bring success in the future election. The queen's aim was to strengthen her own position in order to build influence later on, which would let her son win the throne. The way to success was to be the excellent marriages of her children, which the queen sought for both in the country as well as abroad, and the building of connections' network which was to be a support for the family during the election. Using the model of her guardian and champion, Louise-Marie Gonzaga-Nevers, who had built a faction consisting of the husbands of her ladies-in-waiting, Marie Casimire decided that the means for strengthening the position of the Sobieski family was to marry off her relatives brought from France to the representatives of the Polish magnate families. However, it turned out that, similarly to the case of Louise-Marie, these techniques of building up the court's faction failed.

It is assumed that Marie Casimire de la Grange d'Arquien was born in 1641 in France, although this date is not certain. She came to Poland in 1646 in the retinue of Louise-Marie Gonzaga, who married King Władysław IV Vasa. As the queen's favourite, she married an exceptionally rich voivode of Sandomierz, John Zamoyski, in 1657, and then John Sobieski, later the Crown's Grand Marshall. In 1674, Sobieski was elected the King of Poland. The couple had four children who lived to adulthood: James, Theresa Kunegunda, Aleksander, and Konstanty.

---

* This article was written courtesy of Prof. Aleksandra Skrzypietz who helped me with gathering sources and provided substantial help, for which I am deeply grateful.

Despite their great careers and being enthroned, the position of both spouses was very difficult from the beginning. It was assumed in the Commonwealth – as everywhere else in Europe – that an individual's influence was directly linked with the position of a family, and John Sobieski did not descend from a family of long traditions. Owing to his father's two marriages and his mother's heritage, the last from the Daniłowicz family, he was very wealthy. However, loneliness was the price he had to pay for a huge inheritance – he did not have any close relatives, apart from his sister Catherine, whose first husband was Władysław Dominik Zasławski-Ostrogski, and the second – Michał Kazimierz Radziwiłł. In turn, Marie Casimire was a foreigner without any connections. Ladies who came with her from France got married very well, but it seems that after the death of Louise-Marie, they stopped cooperating. Two of the highest rank: Klara de Mailly-Lascaris married John Sobieski's competitor, Lithuanian Chancellor Krzysztof Pac, and Katarzyna Gordon married the Crown's Treasurer, Jan Andrzej Morsztyn, who cooperated for some time with Sobieski, but eventually they went their separate ways in 1683.

When John Sobieski was elected a king, voices were immediately spread against recognising Marie Casimire as the queen and granting their children the royal position.[1] Some of the Lithuanian deputies – a group of people competing against Sobieski for a long time – were against Marie Casimire's coronation. The majority of deputies supported Sobieski,[2] but it became immediately clear that Marie Casimire would have to take up a fight for her place by her husband's side. The king also understood that any attack on his wife would weaken his own position.

Marie Casimire was aware of the balance of power in the Polish-Lithuanian Commonwealth . She was brought up here, and she received political education under the supervision of Queen Louise-Marie. Her marriages, both the first and the second one, were to serve the purposes pursued by the queen and to keep her husbands in the orbit of French influence. After the queen's death, Marie Casimire was actively supporting Duke d'Enghien's candidature to the Polish throne, and when it was taken by Michał Korybut Wiśniowiecki, she tried to stay in agreement with the ruler, even though her husband was the head of the opposition. The aim of the couple's double game in this rivalry taking place in Poland was to secure their position.[3] In 1674, when the fate of the new election was at stake, Marie Casimire acted in favour of her husband's candidature. This does not mean that she played a key role in his success, but she most certainly acted as an intermediary in contacting

1 Woliński 1952, pp. 7–8, 11, 35.

2 *Archiwum spraw zagranicznych francuskie do dziejów Jana Trzeciego: Lata 1674–1677. Akta historyczne do objaśnienia rzeczy polskich służące od roku 1508 do roku 1795.* Coll. by K. Waliszewski. vol. 1. Kraków 1879, p. 219; *Dwa diariusze sejmów warszawskich w 1674 roku odprawionych.* Ed. by F. Kluczycki. Kraków 1881, p. 66.

3 Komaszyński 1983, p. 11.

the French ambassador who, probably after her intervention, decided to allocate the funds he had brought from France to strengthen Sobieski.[4]

At the time when John Sobieski became the king, Marie Casimire was not a very young woman. She was over thirty; she did not have to get used to the Polish culture and customs, which she knew very well; she was not forced to get to know the network existing at her husband's court since she shaped it together with him, however, only to the extent which the new monarch was expected to do it in the Commonwealth. It is worth pointing out that the newly elected king took over the court of his predecessor, because due to the lifetime of offices in Poland, did not have any greater influence on the composition of his circle. He could wait for the death of the officials and appoint his own candidates in their place or seize the first available chance to change their position, giving them other – always higher – functions, but also in this case he had to wait for any vacant place to appear.

After a long delay at the beginning of 1676, John III's and Marie Casimire's coronation took place. It was prevented neither by the opposition's resistance, nor by an advanced pregnancy. Marie Casimire arrived in Cracow from distant Ruthenia, carried all the way in a litter, so as not to harm a child, and she took part in an extended ceremony.[5] Children of the royal couple were also presented during the ceremony, James and two younger daughters, who died shortly after.[6] The decision was made that John III's children would enjoy the prerogatives previously given to children of the other Polish rulers.[7]

The future of their offspring became the greatest problem for the Sobieski couple. The father's elevation to the throne meant that their future was called into question – sons of rulers were not allowed to hold any offices in Poland, which forced them to the lack of influence and made it practically impossible to create any clientele, so important for building political position. They could try to get the crown, but only via the election process, and this required strong support. Wishing to build it, Marie Casimire – following in the footsteps of Marie Louise-Marie, her mentor and tutor – tried to use the politics of marriage.[8] Willing to expand her influence in order to secure her children's future, she was building a network of connections by getting her family involved. Excellent marriages of relatives and acquiring the favour of kinsmen were to give the royal family a stronger position in life as well as after the king's death.[9]

---

4 Skrzypietz 2011, p. 65.

5 Komaszyński 1983, pp. 95–99.

6 Matwijowski 1989, p. 269

7 *Volumina Legum*, pp. 143, 144; Jemiołowski 2000, p. 442; Matwijowski 1976, p. 27.

8 Augustyniak 1999, pp. 147–148; Staszewski 1986, p. 89.

9 Skrzypietz 2013, p. 112.

Having no certainty about her son's future in the face of the Polish throne eligibility, John III demanded from Louis XIV, as his ally, to confer on James duchies and peerages in France, so that they could serve to the prince as a safety measure in case he did not get the Polish crown. This could also elevate James Sobieski's significance and position in the Commonwealth.[10] This demand was not complied by the Sun King, but the idea returned later in a slightly different form.

The queen, very sensitive about her native family but aware of the benefits she and her relatives could provide to each other, started to bring them from France. Anne Louis Arquien de la Grange, Count of Maligny, who accompanied John Sobieski on his war campaigns, stayed in Poland as early as 1670. He played an important role in 1683 when Prince James was entrusted to his care during the march across Hungary. The sixteen-year-old son's participation in the campaign was of great concern to the queen, but the company of the uncle – an experienced soldier – was to alleviate her worries, although according to the prince's letters, he had not been safe all the time.[11]

In 1676 two of Marie Casimire's sisters came to Poland, unmarried Marie Anne and Louis Marie whose husband, François–Gaston de Béthune, Marquis de Chabris, was twice – in 1676 – 1681 and 1686 – 1692 the representative of Louis XIV at the Polish court. Louise Marie accompanied the queen during her frequent travels, and the marchioness' son remained at the court after his parents' departure in 1692, probably counting on making a career by his aunt's side; he forfeited his ecclesiastical career, most likely hoping that Marie Casimire would help him arrange his future better.[12] These hopes turned out to be futile.

The queen's younger sister, Marie Anne, wanted to become a nun, but Marie Casimire brought her to Poland and was looking for a fiancée for her, and finally, in 1678, she married her off to Jan Wielopolski. In 1677 the fiancé became the Deputy Chancellor and one year later – the Grand Chancellor of the Crown. The marriage seemed to be beneficial to both parties, but it soon turned out that neither the sister nor the brother-in-law wished to further cooperate with the court. Wielopolski had received the highest office, and his further career in the system of the Commonwealth was already practically impossible, so he was ready neither to strengthen John III nor to support his wife. In 1684, he went to France on a diplomatic mission, but – despite the queen's instructions – he had no intentions to solicit the hand of Louis XIV's cousin for Prince James. After his return, he joined the anti-royal opposition, and when his home was searched for the proof of treason

10 *Archiwum spraw zagranicznych...* vol. 1, p. 74.

11 James Sobieski to Marie Casimire, [n.p., n.d.]. in: *Listy Jana Sobieskiego do żony Maryi Kazimiry wraz z listami tej królewskiej rodziny i innych znakomitych osób.* Zapis Konstantego Świdzińskiego. *Biblioteka ordynacji Myszkowskich, zapis Konstantego Świdzińskiego.* Kraków 1860. pp. 439–440.

12 Sarnecki 1958 , p. 33.

after his death, Marie Anne had burnt his documents. Therefore, the attempt to win over the supporters through the sister's marriage was unsuccessful.

In 1678. Marie Casimire brought to Poland also her father, Henry de la Grange, Marquis of Arquien, which caused historians' accusations that she cared more for him than for her own children.[13] Meanwhile, as proven by Aleksandra Skrzypietz, apart from the desire to gather the father and siblings around her, the aim of the queen's activities was to benefit from their French background in order to secure her own children's future. The uncertainty of the future of the royal offspring in the Polish-Lithuanian Commonwealth – for one of the ruler's descendants had to win the elections in order for his family to maintain the royal status – kept Marie Casimire up at night. Therefore, she solicited Louis XIV to elevate her father to the position of a duke and a peerage, at the same time securing the right to inherit these titles by her eldest son.[14] This was a slightly modified plan that the family of Sobieski had already previously presented to Louis XIV, but also, this time, they were not heard.

The rivalry was taking place in Europe at that time between France and Habsburgs, which the Polish-Lithuanian Commonwealth could have benefited from through skillfully pursued diplomatic game. However, it turned out that the weakness of the country shaken by the opposition's fights with the subsequent rulers prevented such actions. Throughout John III's entire reign, both parties – the emperor and the King of France – followed the events in Poland very closely. Marie Casimire's pro-Habsburgs plans vexed the French representatives in Poland, who reported that John III was preparing money for repurchasing Silesia from the emperor's hands. Slightly later the French diplomats were very concerned that the queen was soliciting the emperor to sell the rights to one of the Silesian duchies to her father, and he would leave them as an inheritance for Prince James. These territories could have been a support in the dynastic plans of the Sobieski family and make it easier for the prince to win the throne.[15] The cash injection which Leopold I would have received from this were also triggering French concern.

The presence of Marie Casimire's relatives at her court facilitated the contact with the queen to the envoys from France. In 1693 a new French ambassador, Melchior de Polignac, wrote that thanks to Marquis d'Arquien's intermediation, he had managed to unofficially meet the queen even before he had gone to an audience with the king.[16] The queen's father was becoming a go-between in providing access to her. Perhaps it was due to these services and the willingness to improve the relations between Poland and France that Louis XIV awarded the marquis with

13 Konopczyński 1921, p. 79; Żeleński-Boy 1974, p. 239.

14 *Archiwum spraw zagranicznych...*, vol. 1, p. 476.

15 *Archiwum spraw zagranicznych...*, vol. 2, p. 360; Komaszyński 1983, pp. 110–111.

16 TW, no. 8726, pp. 5028–5035.

the order of the Holy Spirit in 1694, which Marie Casimire – always sensitive to honours – greatly appreciated.[17]

The greatest honour was bestowed upon the marquis in 1695 when he received – at the queen's request – a cardinal's hat from Innocent XII. The aim was to encourage her to opt for Poland to remain in the anti-Turkish league, and fighting against Turkey was no longer providing the country with any tangible benefits. John III did not want to abandon the alliance despite the encouragement from France, and the Pope acted in favour of the Habsburgs and Venice. It can be said that the rivalry between France and the Habsburgs taking place in Europe benefitted Cardinal d'Arquien, since Louis XIV granted him a salary of 20 thousand livres, which wholly satisfied Marie Casimire,[18] even though she had no sufficient influence on her husband's decision regarding the end or continuation of the war against Turkey.

The marriage between Marie Anne de la Grange d'Arquien and Jan Wielkopolski did not bring benefits to the Sobieski couple, but the children of Marchioness de Béthune arrived at the royal court, and the queen decided to try the dynastic politics once again. In 1691, Marie Catherine de Béthune married the Grand Marshall of Lithuania, Stanisław Kazimierz Radziwiłł, not the youngest one for he was born in 1648 and had already reached the top of his career. Marrying off the female cousins to magnates of high rank gave a chance that if they turned out to be loyal, their influence would have been more precious than that of young men who were starting their careers and were dependent on their older relatives.

In the case of Marie Catherine, the queen was most likely relying not only on winning her husband over to the court's politics, but she probably also assumed that her niece would receive a considerable fortune, which would provide her with good circumstances for the next marriage. Radziwiłł did, in fact, die towards the end of this year, and the queen immediately found another candidate to Marie Catherine's hand. Not even a year of the traditional mourning had passed when the widow married Aleksander Paweł Sapieha, who was awarded the office of the Court Marshall of Lithuania.[19] He belonged to the most important family in Lithuania, right next to the family of Radziwiłł, and turned out to be willing to cooperate with the Sobieskis, keeping his own benefits in mind.

In 1691 the queen's second niece, Joanne, married the Crown's Standard-bearer, Jan Stanisław Jabłonowski,[20] a young man standing at the threshold of his career, a son of the Grand Hetman of the Crown, once a companion of John III who, however, had been keeping distance from the court for a long time.

---

17 Ziembicki 1934, p. 17.

18 „Gazette de France", Varsovie, 11 II 1696, 17 III 1696, 31 III 1696; Forst battaglia 1983, p. 368; Komaszyński 1983, p. 165.

19 Marie Casimire to James Sobieski, Jaworów, 27 IV [?], NGAB f. 694, o. 12, ms 151, c. 14r–17v.

20 Sarnecki 1958 , pp. 235.

Count de Maligny's son, the queen's nephew, was also staying at the court, he accompanied the young Sobieskis, but he had his own plans and wished to marry one of Radziwiłł's daughters.[21] The project failed because it was unthinkable for a high-ranked family to marry off their daughter to a poor Frenchman. For it was one thing to welcome foreign women to one's house and another to force one's own daughter to an uncertain future with a poor foreigner.

Matrimonial relationships with the magnates could be a way to form a court party and to give strong support to the royal politics. This way, Marie Casimire wanted to acquire the wealthiest families in Poland for her own purposes, the benefits were to be mutual though not obvious, and the marriages arranged by the queen did not always go well. Jan Stanisław Jabłonowski was to treat his wife badly, perhaps feeling that he was manoeuvred into this relationship, and he had to wait two years for the next promotion to the voivode of Volhynia, even though right after the wedding he strove for the voivodeship of Malbork.[22] In turn, the Sapieha family benefited considerably, but their influence and expectations were also greater.

A serious strife took place in 1695 due to the kinship and affinities with the Sobieski family. In spring, the Comonwealth was shaken by the conflict over the care of properties of the late Ludwika Karolina Radziwiłł, who orphaned her daughter Elisabeth Auguste Sofie of Palatinate-Neuburg. The families of Radziwiłł and Sapieha argued about the management of her vast wealth,[23] and soon the conflict reached the royal court. John III was a relative of the Radziwiłł family, but Marie Casimire supported the Sapieha family, who was related to her.[24] For this reason, scandalous scenes took place between the royal couple because John III spoke in favour of the nephew, Karol Stanisław Radziwiłł, the Lithuanian Vice-chancellor, and the queen supported Aleksander Paweł Sapieha, her niece's husband.[25] The Sapieha family was also supported by the Lubomirski family, so it seemed that the queen's activities had a broader scope. It is unknown whether the disagreements between the royal spouses were sincere; perhaps they were only pretending in order to convince the fighting parties that they had the royal family's support. Regardless of the conflict's outcome, the victorious family would be willing to show gratitude for the king's or the queen's support. The decision regarding the management of Radziwiłł's properties was made in the Lithuanian Tribunal,[26] but it was believed that it was influenced by the father of the underage heiress, Charles III Philip of

21 Ibidem, pp. 99, 127–129, 140, 144, 332.

22 Popiołek 2003, p. 199.

23 Kazimierz Sapieha to John III, Vilnius, [??] 1695, AGAD AR II ms 32, ff. 10–11.

24 Sarnecki 1958, pp. 291, 293–294, 297–298.

25 Kazimierz Sarnecki to Karol Stanisław Radziwiłł, Warsaw, 22 VIII 1695, AGAD, AR V no. 13939.

26 Jabłonowski 1865, pp. 96–97.

Palatine-Neuburg, or rather his sister, Empress Eleonore of Palatinate-Neuburg.[27] It was her that the Sapieha family turned to for help, and they were successful.

The queen who supported the Sapieha family knew how to exert some influence on them. In March 1695, during the greatest tension in Lithuania, she skilfully encouraged Aleksander Sapieha to remain, together with his wife, in Warsaw by the king's side. Summoned by his father, Sapieha packed the carriages and planned to go to Lithuania with his pregnant wife. Marie Casimire claimed that her niece would have safer childbirth under the royal doctors' care. Sapieha opposed pleading the lack of money, but the queen promised to pay for their stay in the capital.[28] Rejecting the queen's offer probably during the conflict over Radziwiłł's properties would have been a mistake, so the couple stayed at court.

Slightly earlier, Marie Casimire tried to play a role in selecting a husband for John III's niece, Teofila Zasławska-Ostrogska, who, as a seventeen-year-old, married the Great Crown Hetman, Dymitr Wiśniowiecki, the enemy of John Sobieski. This marriage did not improve the relationship between Sobieski and Wiśniowiecki, and it was not the most successful until the moment when after the death of her brother, Aleksander, Teofila inherited the enormous property of the Ostrogski ordination. She became a widow in 1682, and the queen wished to marry her off to her brother, Anne Louis d'Arquien. However, Teofila waited until the end of the mourning period and married Józef Karol Lubormiski who received, together with her hand, all the estates of her brother and her first husband. Wiśniowiecki's relatives took up the fight for the inheritance, and John III was not able to help and to support his niece; at one point, she was even sentenced to exile for breaking court sentences. Her marriage to Józef Karol Lubomirski could have turned out to be beneficial to the royal family because he was the representative of the influential family, whose acquisition could have been very important. For this reason, both spouses frequented the court as guests. In 1692 Lubomirski became the Court Marshall of the Crown, i.e. the most important official at the royal court, and his wife regularly came to the capital to visit her husband and mother, Catherine Radziwiłł, who was widowed and spent a lot of time with her royal brother. The Court Marshall's wife arrived in court also for childbirth, and stayed there under the care of her mother, the queen, ladies-in-waiting, and the best physicians.[29]

It should be emphasised that Marie Casimire not only used her relatives and in-laws but also built good relationships with them. In 1674 when she was expecting a child, her malaise and physicians' pessimistic opinions made her ask her sister-in-law, Catherine Radziwiłł, to take care of her two daughters and the newborn baby in

---

27 James Sobieski do Eleonore, [n. p, n. d.]. NGAB f. 694, o. 12, ms 376, c. 45; NN to Leopold I, [n.p.], 12 IV 1695, HHSTA, Polen ms I/82, f. 43r; Schmidt 1963, p. 26; Sliesoriūnas 2000, p. 174.

28 Sarnecki 1958, pp. 37, 102, 104, 137, 235, 293.

29 Skrzypietz 2019, pp. 61–74.

case of her death. She claimed that the sister-in-law was the closest person to her,[30] and she feared that children would suffer under the care of a stepmother.[31] Slightly earlier, when Marie Casimire had left for France before the election of her husband, she took care there of Catherine's son from her first marriage, Aleksander Zasławski-Ostrogski,[32] assuring his mother that he was "healthy and behaves well".[33] In the 1690s Catherine was a frequent guest at the royal court, she entertained sick John III, she went with Marie Casimire to churches and for walks. This could bring the royal couple closer to the nephew of the Vice-Chancellor of Lithuania, Karol Stanisław Radziwiłł,[34] and become a means of influencing him.

Great marriages were a way to secure the future of Marie Casimire's children, and they were the aim of her efforts. In 1677, she made contact with Radziwiłłs, making plans to get for her the then ten-year-old son a hand of equally young Ludwika Karolina, an heiress of grand estates of the line of Birże and Dubinki.[35] Radziwiłł's fortune would become a political base in the form of a numerous clientele.[36] The opposition overthrew these projects, hiding behind the young lady's age, but John III – to his own disappointment – also did not come across any help from his sister who belonged to another line of Radziwiłłs through marriage.[37] In 1687, the plans of marrying James Sobieski off to Ludwika Karolina Radziwiłł – at that time already a widow of the son of Elector of Brandenburg, Margrave Louis – returned.[38] Marie Casimire got involved in these efforts.[39] She ordered a carriage and horses, jewellery, dresser, and many other gifts for the son's fiancée, but she was worried about the outcome of these efforts.[40] Therefore, she sought the help of Catherine Radziwiłł, but did not meet with understanding and help.[41] The margravine did not keep the word given to the prince, and she married Charles Philip of Palatinate-Neuburg.[42]

Marie Casimire was searching for the candidates for her son's wife also at the royal courts of Louis XIV and Leopold I.[43] In 1680 the king's brother-in-law, Vice-

30 Marie Casimire to Catherine Radziwiłł, [n.p., n.d.]. in: Niemcewicz 1839, p. 360.

31 Marie Casimire to Catherine Radziwiłł, [n.p., n.d.]. in: Niemcewicz 1839, p. 363; Marie Casimire to Catherine Radziwiłł, [n.p., n.d.]. in: Niemcewicz 1839, p. 366.

32 Jan Sobieski 1962, p. 287.

33 Marie Casimire to Catherine Radziwiłł, [n.p., n.d.]. in: Niemcewicz 1839, p. 368.

34 Skrzypietz 2019, pp. 61–74.

35 Komaszyński 1983, p. 110.

36 TL no. 2998 /I, p. 66; Wójcik 1994, pp. 254–268.

37 John III to Catherine Radziwiłł [n.p.] 14 VIII 1680, BPAN ms 949, f. 194.

38 Komaszyński 1983, p. 125; Piwarski 1929, p. 10.

39 Ziembicki 1934, pp. 8–10.

40 Ibidem, p. 14.

41 Bartoszewicz 1935, p. 87.

42 Forst battaglia 1983, p. 315; Helcel 1857, p. 70.

43 Skrzypietz 2011, pp. 168–177.

Chancellor of Lithuania, Michał Kazimierz Radziwiłł, was to seek for the hand of an archduchess for Prince James, but he proved himself neither in sufficient skills nor in initiative.[44] The plan of such marriage was doomed to fail from the beginning, but still the kinship with the Sobieski family did not encourage Radziwiłł to any greater efforts. Similarly, in 1685 Marie Casimire's brother-in-law, the Crown Chancellor Jan Wielopolski, was to woo for the hand of the French princess for Prince James; the royal couple dreamt of Louis XIV's niece, Élisabeth-Charlotte Lady of Chartres.[45] However, Wielopolski did not make any greater efforts, and, consequently, his mission gave no expected results.[46]

The relatives and kinsmen not always could or wanted to help the Sobieski couple in pursuing their ambitions, but it also happened that they tried to sabotage them. Marquise de Béthune was a representative loyal to his policymaker, Louis XIV, and not to his sister-in-law, but wishing to alleviate Marie Casimire's discontentment regarding the troubles in finding the appropriate candidate for the wife of Prince James, he tried to divert her attention and anger, deluding her with how Theresa Kunegunda could marry the nephew of Louis XIV, Philip, Duke of Chartres.[47] He explained that this duke's sister, Mademoiselle de Chartres, could only get married to a king, and the prince's route to the throne was unsure.[48] In turn, he proposed a princess of Hanover,[49] but this did not go along with the queen's projects, because she was looking for a family that would significantly help Sobieski at the election. Desperate Marie Casimire was met with understanding by the Roman Curia and the imperial court, where it was recognised that any further rejections of her plans would end in John III' resignation from the Holy League; if Louis XIV inclined towards the queen's wishes, the alliance would be threatened. It does not matter whether this kind of political change was possible, but the very concerns were enough, there is no doubt that the prince's French marriage could cause troubles to the Habsburgs. Therefore, in 1691 the marriage was finalised between Prince James and Hedwig Elisabeth of Palatinate-Neuburg. The fiancée was from a low-ranked but very well connected family and her sister was the empress. The Sobieski couple had to pay a great wedding gift, and the emperor secured the money in Oława, situated in Silesia, where the Prince James took refuge with his family after losing the election of 1697.[50]

---

44 *Archiwum spraw zagranicznych...*, vol. 2, p. 81,289; Piwarski 1938, p. 14.

45 François-Louis de Béthune to Marie Casimire, [n.p. n.d.], NGAB f. 694, o. 12, ms 248, f. 16r-v.

46 Forst battaglia 1983, pp. 280–281.

47 Ibidem, pp. 327–328.

48 Wójcik 1994, p. 459.

49 TL no. 3002 /I, pp. 96, 103–105; TW no. 8725, p. 3732.

50 Skrzypietz 2015, pp. 288–291.

The news about the preparations for marriage caused the Versailles' concern, and for that reason Marquis de Béthune tried to prevent its finalisation by getting in touch with the anti-royal opposition in Poland,[51] threatening that Prince James' marriage will strengthen the position of the Sobieski family and will lead to the throne succession.[52] He also tried to change Marie Casimire's attitude to her son's relationship, promising benefits to her family.[53] Additionally, he was spreading rumours that the marriage would end in failure because Marie Casimire would interfere with the young couple's life.[54] Marquis d'Arquien – most likely egged on by Marquis de Béthune – was also against this marriage. However, the Palatine princess ultimately arrived in Warsaw where she was welcomed by Catherine Radziwiłł and Marie Casimire's both sisters, Marie Louise de Béthune and Marie Anne Wielopolska.[55] All three were also a part of the wedding procession which led the bride from Ujazdów to Warsaw.[56] The Sobieski couple made sure that their daughter-in-law made two ceremonial entries, one when she travelled from Silesia to Warsaw – and many ceremonial meetings, entries, and feasts took place along the way – and the second one when she was brought to Saint John's Church, in which she was married.[57] However, the king's and queen's sisters did not attend the wedding feast due to the disputes over the places they should take. As the closest relatives, they wanted to sit close to the royal couple, but it was required that they take seats in accordance with their position in the hierarchy of senatorial wives. For the same reason, the queen's father also did not attend the feast since he wished to sit in a higher place than the papal nuncio, and he did not receive this seat.[58]

By turning to the members of her family, bringing them to Poland, and then searching for fiancés for her sister and nieces, Marie Casimire tried to introduce them to the Polish elite circles. Securing their future, she hoped to use these connections in politics. The families that were won over should strengthen her husband's reign but – first and foremost – support her son during the election. Undertaking these actions, the queen followed in the footsteps of her tutor, Louise-Marie, who – by arranging marriages of her ladies-in-waiting – was building the royal and pro-French faction, and she used Marie Casimire twice, marrying her off richly and

51 François-Louis de Béthune to Colbert de Croissy, Żółkiew, 8 XI 1689, HHSTA Polen, ms I/81, ff. 11–11a.

52 TW, no. 8725, pp. 3947, 3949, 3959, 3965–3966, 4002, 4031, 4074.

53 [?] Clotomont to Marie Casimire, Paris, 21.07.1690, HHSTA, Polen ms I/81, f. 4.

54 Załęski 1908, p. 118.

55 TL no. 3003 /I, p. 16; „Gazette de France", 28 IV 1691; *Opis historyczny zaślubin królewica polskiego Jakuba Sobieskiego*, ed. Aleksander Wejnert, Warszawa 1851, p. 16.

56 Ibidem, p. 16.

57 *Diariusz podróży elektorowej Bawarii z Warszawy do Brukseli.* In: M. Komaszyński, *Teresa Kunegunda Sobieska*, Warszawa 1982, p. 294.

58 Ibidem, p. 293.

profitably. Marie Casimire fulfilled the plans of her patroness, she also became convinced this was the right and fruitful way of achieving benefits. The transaction was interchangeable because both sides – the queen and the magnates gained through marriages – were to provide services to each other, but ultimately, Marie Casimire was not successful in implementing these plans of cooperation. It seems she did not draw conclusions from the behaviour of her sister, Marie Anne Wielopolska, who was not loyal towards her even after the death of her husband. None of the magnates won over by the queen was willing to help in the efforts made by her for the benefit of her offspring. They did not want to help her in finding a good match for her son since this would strengthen the influence of the Sobieski family, and each of those families could dream about the crown on their own heads. Another Sobieski on the throne would pose a threat to the Polish election, and although the spectre of establishing a dynasty and introducing an absolute rule was unrealistic, this threat was still present in the political propaganda. The only role that Marie Casimire's relatives and kinsmen played at the royal court were their representational functions, and even those were not taken when they felt threatened in their right to precedence, linking their unique positions with the kinship with the royal couple. They could also play the role of go-betweens in the contacts with the queen, but there is not a lot of evidence for it in the sources. None of them sided with James Sobieski during the election after the death of John III. It can be assumed that by weaving a net of affinities, Marie Casimire – probably involuntarily – served to a great extent to her relatives and kinsmen than her children, though it was not her goal.

Bibliography

Archive sources

AGAD AR = Archiwum Główne Akt Dawnych Archiwum Radziwiłłów, Warsaw, II ms 32.

AGAD AR = Archiwum Główne Akt Dawnych Archiwum Radziwiłłów, Warsaw, V ms 13939.

BPAN = Biblioteka Naukowa PAN i PAU, Cracow, ms 949.

HHSTA = Haus- Hof- und Staats Archiv, Vienna, Polen ms I/81.

NGAB = Nacyjanalnyj Gistaryczny Archiu Biełarusi, Minsk fond 694, opis 12 ms 151, 376.

TL = Teki Lukasa, Biblioteka Ossolińskich, Wrocław, no. 2998 /I, 3003 /I, 3002/I.

TW = Teki Waliszewskiego, Biblioteka Naukowa PAN i PAU, Cracow, no. 8725, 8726.

Printed sources

Archiwum spraw zagranicznych francuskie do dziejów Jana Trzeciego: Lata 1674–1677. Akta historyczne do objaśnienia rzeczy polskich służące od roku 1508 do roku 1795. ed. Kazimierz Waliszewski, vol. 1, AU, Cracow 1879.

Archiwum spraw zagranicznych francuskie do dziejów Jana Trzeciego: Lata 1677–1679. Akta historyczne do objaśnienia rzeczy polskich służące od roku 1508 do roku 1795, vol. 2, AU, Cracow 1881.

Diariusz podróży elektorowej Bawarii z Warszawy do Brukseli. W: Michał Komaszyński, *Teresa Kunegunda Sobieska*, PIW, Warsaw 1982.

Dwa diariusze sejmów warszawskich w 1674 roku odprawionych, ed. Franciszek Kluczycki, AU, Cracow 1881.

JABŁONOWSKI 1865 = Jan Stanisław Jabłonowski, *Dziennik (1694–1695)*, ed. Władysław Chomętowski, Warsaw 1865.

JAN SOBIESKI 1962 = Jan Sobieski, *Listy do Marysieńki*, ed. Leszek Kukulski, "Czytelnik", Warsaw 1962.

JEMIOŁOWSKI 2000 = Mikołaj Jemiołowski, *Pamiętnik dzieje Polski zawierający (1648–1679)*, coll. by Jan Dzięgielewski, DiG, Warsaw 2000.

Listy Jana Sobieskiego do żony Maryi Kazimiry wraz z listami tej królewskiej rodziny i innych znakomitych osób. Zapis Konstantego Świdzińskiego. *Biblioteka ordynacji Myszkowskich, zapis Konstantego Świdzińskiego.* Cracow 1860.

NIEMCEWICZ 1839 = Julian Ursyn Niemcewicz, *Zbiór pamiętników historycznych o dawnej Polszcze z rękopismów, tudzież dzieł w różnych językach o Polszcze wydanych, oraz z listami oryginalnemi królów i znakomitych ludzi w kraju naszym*, vol. 4, Lipsk 1839.

Opis historyczny zaślubin królewica polskiego Jakuba Sobieskiego, ed. Aleksander Wejnert, "Biblioteka Warszawska", Warsaw 1851.

SARNECKI 1958 = *Pamiętniki z czasów Jana Sobieskiego. Diariusz i relacje z lat 1691–1696*, ed. Janusz Woliński, Zakład Narodowy im. Ossoliński, Wrocław 1958.

Volumina Legum, vol. 5. Wydawnictwa Artystyczne i Filmowe Warsaw 1980.

ZIEMBICKI 1935 = Witold Ziembicki, *Nieznane listy Marii Kazimiery*, Zakład Narodowy im. Ossoliński, Wrocław 1934.

"Gazette de France"

Modern sources

AUGUSTYNIAK 1999 = Urszula Augustyniak, *Wazowie i "królowie rodacy": studium władzy królewskiej w Rzeczypospolitej XVII wieku*, "Semper" Warsaw 1999.

BARTOSZEWICZ 1935 = Julian Bartoszewicz, *Zamek bialski*, Gebethner i Wolff, Warsaw 1935.

FORST DE BATTAGLIA 1983 = Otto Forst de Battaglia, *Jan Sobieski król Polski*, PIW, Warsaw 1983.

Helcel 1857 = Zygmunt Helcel, *O dwukrotnem zamęściu księżniczki Ludwika Karoliny Radziwiłłównej i wynikłych stąd w Polsce zamieszkach. Przyczynek do dziejów panowania Jana III*, Cracow 1857.
Komaszyński 1983 = Michał Komaszyński, *Maria Kazimiera d'Arquien Sobieska królowa Polski (1641–1716)*, Wydawnictwo Literackie, Cracow 1983.
Konopczyński 1921 = Władysław Konopczyński, *Dwie królowe*, in: *Od Sobieskiego do Kościuszki. Szkice - drobiazgi - fraszki historyczne*, Gebetner i Wolff, Warsaw 1921.
Matwijowski 1976 = Krystyn Matwijowski, *Pierwsze sejmy z czasów Jana III Sobieskiego*, Zakład Narodowy im. Ossoliński, Wrocław 1976.
Matwijowski 1989 = Krystyn Matwijowski, *Uroczystości przedkoronacyjne i przyczyny zmiany pierwszego terminu koronacji Jana III Sobieskiego*. In: *Źródłoznawstwo i studia historyczne*. Ed. by Kazimierz Bobowski, Acta Universitatis Wrartislaviensis, Wydawnictwo Uniwersytetu Wrocławskiego, Historia 74. Wrocław 1989.
Piwarski 1929 = Kazimierz Piwarski, *Sprawa pruska za Jana III Sobieskiego (1688–1689)*. "Kwartalnik Historyczny", vol. 63, 1929.
Piwarski 1938 = Kazimierz Piwarski, *Pomysły odzyskania Śląska za Jana III Sobieskiego*, Instytut Śląski, Katowice 1938.
Popiołek 2003 = Bożena Popiołek, *Kobiecy świat w czasach Augusta II. Studia nad mentalnością kobiet z kręgów szlacheckich*, Wydawnictwo Naukowe Akademii Pedagogicznej, Cracow 2003.
Schmidt 1963 = Hans Schmidt, *Kurfürst Karl Philip von der Palatinate als Reichsfürst*. Bibliographisches Institut, Mannheim 1963.
Skrzypietz 2011 = Aleksandra Skrzypietz, *Królewscy synowie - Jakub, Aleksander i Konstanty Sobiescy*, Wydawnictwo Uniwersytetu Śląskiego, Katowice 2011.
Skrzypietz 2013 = Aleksandra Skrzypietz, *Pozycja królewicza polskiego w XVII wieku*, in: *Między Barokiem a Oświeceniem. Społeczeństwo stanowe*, ed. Stanisław Achremczyk, Jerzy Kiełbik, Ośrodek Badań Naukowych im. Wojciecha Kętrzyńskiego: Towarzystwo Naukowe im. Wojciecha Kętrzyńskiego, Olsztyn 2013.
Skrzypietz 2015 = *Jakub Sobieski*, Wydawnictwo Poznański, Poznań 2015.
Skrzypietz 2019 = *Siostra królewska Katarzyna z Sobieskich Radziwiłłowa na dworze Jana III w świetle przekazów Kazimierza Sarneckiego.*W: *Sapientia ars vivendi putanda est. Wokół polityki i kultury. Studia z dziejów nowożytnych ofiarowane Profesorowi Marianowi Chachajowi*, red. A. Perłakowski, F. Wolański, B. Rok, Księgarnia Akademicka, Cracow 2019, s. 61–74.
Sliesoriūnas 2000 = Gintautas Sliesoriūnas, *Lietuvos didžioji kunigaikštystė vidaus karo išvakarėse: didikų grupuočių kova 1690–1697m*, *Lietuvos* istorijos instituto leidykla, Vilnius 2000.
Staszewski 1986 = Jacek Staszewski, *Polacy w osiemnastowiecznym Dreźnie*, Zakład Narodowy im. Ossoliński, Wrocław-Warsaw-Cracow-Gdańsk-Łódź 1986.
Woliński 1952 = Janusz Woliński, *Epilog elekcji 1674 roku*. Rozprawy Wydziału Historyczno-Filozoficznego, series II, vol. 46, no 5, PAU, Cracow 1952.

Wójcik 1994 = Zbigniew Wójcik, *Jan Sobieski (1629–1696)*, PIW, Warsaw 1994.

Załęski 1908 = Stanisław Załęski, *Jezuici w Polsce*, L. Anczyc, Cracow 1908.

Żeleński-Boy 1974 = Tadeusz Żeleński-Boy, *Marysieńka Sobieska*, PIW, Warsaw 1974.

Aleksandra Skrzypietz

Maria Clementina Sobieska in a Web of Court Intrigues

Abstract:
Maria Clementina Sobieska, the granddaughter of John III Sobieski, was born and raised in Oława. Her father, Prince James, lost his chance for the crown and political influence. Legends circulated around Europe about the wealth of the Sobieski family and the great dowries of the royal granddaughters. Of even greater importance were the family connections through her mother, Hedwig Elisabeth of Palatinate-Neuburg, whose sisters sat on a few European thrones and brothers in the Palatinate and the Reich's bishoprics. For this reason, Maria Clementina was chosen as the wife of James Stuart, the titular King of England. Hope for his return to the throne occurs a few times, which was strengthened by the support from France and then Spain. A close kinship between Sobieska and the Queen of Spain, Elisabeth Farnese, could have played a key role in these efforts. Despite obstacles, the marriage took place in 1719, but it soon turned out that any hopes associated with it were vanishing. It was recognized at the Stuart court that the queen had no rights to her own judgements and decisions. Her spouse did not arrange a separate court for her, he entrusted her with the supervision of their son, and then – definitely prematurely – he handed him over to men and surrounded him with people who Maria Clementina did not tolerate. Sobieska's role came down to representative functions only. James Stuart's microscopic court was shaken by intrigues and faction divisions, and the queen became entangled in the game played there, opposing the influences of her husband's favourites. Her opposition to them led to a breakdown of her marriage. Sobieska's decision to leave for the convent surprised everyone who observed for a few years how with sadness, but without any open protest, she had yielded to her husband's will and to the influence of his favourites.

Maria Clementina Sobieska (1701–1735), the daughter of Prince James Sobieski and Hedwig Elisabeth of Palatinate-Neuburg, was the granddaughter of the Polish King, John III Sobieski. After the lost election in 1697, the prince lived in Oława in Silesia, where on the 17th of July 1701 his fourth daughter – the father's favourite – was born.[1] The queen dowager, Marie Casimire, dreamt of having all her granddaughters become queens, and she strived for their excellent marriages. Legends

1 Konstanty Sobieski to Alexander Sobieski, Oława, 17 VII 1701, NGAB, fond 694, opis 12, ms 350, ff. 116–117.

circulated around Europe about the wealth of John III, and thus, James Stuart, the King of England *de iure*, became interested in the princesses due to their dowry and connections. In 1718, Charles Wogan went on reconnaissance to Oława, and in the spring, the marriage contract was signed on behalf of James Stuart by James Murray.[2] The princess was given nearly 2 million zloty in dowry; these were sums placed in the Paris city hall and debts that the Polish treasury owed to the Sobieski family, but acquiring them back turned out to be difficult.[3]

The fiancée was also desirable because of her extended European connections. Her first cousin was Elisabeth Farnese, the Queen of Spain, and in 1719, Spain was helping Stuart to return to the throne of his ancestors. The Holy Roman Emperor – also the first cousin of Maria Clementina – was allied with George I and imprisoned her when she was on her way to her fiancé; James Stuart showered his bride with assurances about his feelings and urged her to persevere by his side.[4] Therefore, Sobieska refuted the offers of other marriages, and Charles Wogan freed her through deception,[5] most likely with the quiet consent of the Emperor,[6] and took her to Bologna. This is where she married Stuart *per procura*. Despite her young age, Murray praised the princess' maturity, "her feelings, reasoning, assessment of affairs, her behaviour and actions [...]."[7] He vouched that the king could not wish for a better wife. Maria Clementina was accompanied in Bologna by Eleanor Misset, who helped to transport her from Innsbruck, and Marjorie Hay, the sister of James Murray.[8] While seeking that his sister could serve Maria Clementina, Murray assured the king that Marjorie had won her favour.[9] At the same time, Murray tried to take control of the queen's contacts,[10] when she tried to get to know all the people from her husband's circles, and therefore James Stuart's secretary, David Nairne, complained that Murray did not allow him for the meeting with Maria Clementina.[11]

Upon her arrival in Rome, the queen took up residence in the convent of the Ursuline nuns. She was visited by English ladies accompanied by their husbands. Maria Clementina – accustomed to the closeness of women: mother, sisters, their

---

2 James Stuart do James Sobieski, [n.p., n.d.], RA SP Main/32, ff.30–32.

3 Marriage contract of Maria Clementina and James Stuart, Oława, 23 VII 1718, AGAD AR II, ms 2387, ff. 1–7.

4 Szajnocha 1909, p. 8.

5 Wogan 1894, passim; Miller 1968, pp. 54–55;

6 Gürtler 1991, p. 10.

7 James Murray to James Stuart, [n.p.] 20 VI 1719, RA SP Main/43, ff. 123–124.

8 Maria Clementina to James Sobieski, Rome, 20. 05.1719, NGAB f. 694, o. 12, ms 358, ff. 50r-52v.

9 James Murray to James Stuart, [n.p.] 1 VIII 1719, RA SP MAIN/43, f. 26.

10 Corp 2011, p. 132.

11 Corp 2018, pp. 366, 367.

large female circle and ladies coming to Oława – would have been more uninhibited, but Stuart's court was masculinised. Lost in the new environment – similarly to many other princesses in her situation – Sobieska complained to her father that she felt insecure.[12] She wrote to the absent husband: "I do not doubt your kindness and care which are the greatest consolation to me in the uncertainty, in which I have found myself again".[13]

The spouses met on the 3rd of September in Montefiascone. Murray appointed Maria Clementina's retinue, in which not a single person from the servants who had come from Oława was present, and he also insisted that these people return to Silesia and be dismissed.[14] The court's financial problems were the reason for their departure, but this argument always appeared when one wanted to cut queens off from the support of renowned people and take control of their circles.

There was a struggle for influence alongside James Stuart, and the Jacobites were getting divided into factions, and Maria Clementina was at the centre of this rivalry; no royal court was free from such struggles. A monarch should appease anxieties and resolve misunderstandings, but it turned out that James Stuart could not play the role of an arbiter and to rise above the tensions troubling the court, which weakened his position. The more he declared he wanted to be the only lord in his household,[15] the less he was becoming one, and James Murray, together with Marjorie and John Hay, enjoyed the greatest influence at his court.[16] The king trusted James Murray and appointed him as the secretary of state, although he was obnoxious towards the queen and even the cardinals.[17] John Hay became the *maggiordomo*, and both brother-in-law held the highest offices at the court. Soon after Maria Clementina's arrival, unrest started between the Jacobites in Rome. Marjorie Hay and her brother offended with their behaviour many people associated with the court; their greed for power and conceit alienated almost everyone except the king. Perhaps the Jacobites were emboldened by the queen's arrival, which could change the balance of power in the court.

Maria Clementina's circles included people who were chosen by the king. Everyone she knew, together with people who had helped her to run away from Innsbruck, we dismissed except for Eleanor Misset,[18] and James Stuart had previously stated

12 Maria Clementina to James Sobieski, Rome, 3 VI 1719, NGAB f. 694, o. 12, ms 358, ff. 55r-56v.

13 Maria Clementina to James Stuart, Rome, 15 VIII 1719, RA SP Main/44 ff. 49–50.

14 Corp 2011, pp. 132, 369, 381.

15 James Stuart to Maria Clementina, Rome, 9 XI 1725, RA SP Main/87, ff. 64–65.

16 Daiches 1973, pp. 78–79; Niemojowska 1992, pp. 113, 137–138; Shield, Lang 1907, p. 369.

17 Corp 2018, pp. 371,374.

18 Maria Clementina to James Sobieski, Montefiascone, 20 IX 1719, NGAB f. 694, o. 12, ms 358, c. 88r-89v; Wogan 1894, pp. 37–38.

that his wife should not promise a place at court to anyone without his consent.[19] She also was not given a separate household, allegedly due to the fact that her husband had small an income. Maria Clementina had a servant, washerwoman, needlewoman, butler and an elderly butler, the only one man from Oława. The royal couple shared physicians and confessor.[20] It is not known if the secretary, Robert Creagh, previously an undersecretary of Murray,[21] was given to the queen as a spy, or if this resulted from the court's paucity, but he was probably loyal to her.[22] The queen's chambermaids were sisters Mary Fitzgerald and Isabella Gordon, and their brother Alexander – her servant; the Gordon siblings were the cousins of the king's secretary, David Nairne,[23] who was in contact with John Erskine, Duke of Mar.

The queen also needed ladies-in-waiting, but James Murray had the female representatives of aristocracy removed from her; Frances Erskine, Duchess of Mar, and Mary Keith, Countess of Marischal, were to enter her closest circles, but together with Winifred Maxwell, Countess Nithsdale, they were all removed, which triggered dissatisfaction among some of the Jacobites. Only Marjorie Hay stayed with the queen, but – contrary to her brother's opinions – she did not manage to win her trust. Eleanor Misset and female servants became Maria Clementina's – quite unsuitable – companions. There was no one in her circles of a higher social rank. She did not have a chamberlain who would accompany her during journeys, announce guests, and perform representative tasks. She also did not have a lady-in-waiting who should stay with her and add splendour to her royal position. Belonging to the close queen's circle, accompanying her was not only an honour to the ladies of high ranks , but also gave them specific influence, by having direct access to the queen, facilitating meetings with her, and also by having influence on decisions made at royal courts. Regardless of the actual participation of the female monarch in power, the position of *lady-in-waiting* in England, *dame-d'honneur* in France, or in Poland, was highly desired. In the meantime, apart from Winifred Maxwell, Countess Nithsdale, negatively seen by James Stewart, and Marjorie Hay, there were no ladies in Sobieska's circles.[24]

It was most likely Eleanor Misset who played a role of an intermediary between the queen and Jacobites from France, where lived gathered the enemies of John Hay and James Murray – General Arthur Dillon, John Erskine, Duke of Mar, and George Granville, Lord Lansdowne. A circle of people averse to the king's favourites was created around Maria Clementina, which triggered the king's dissatisfaction, as he

19 James Stuart to Maria Clementina, Rome, 7 II 1719, RA SP Main/41, ff. 14–15.

20 Corp 2011, pp. 126–127,132,134

21 Corp 2018, pp. 385,391.

22 Robert Creagh's correspondence, NGAB, f. 694, o. 12, ms 333.

23 Corp 2018, p. 391.

24 Corp 2011, p. 134.

was certain about their goodwill and importance. Staying under their overwhelming influence, James Stuart started to see his own wife as a threat since she opposed their influence. Opposition to James Murray and John Hay coming from France and Britain was serious; when the king was looking for candidates for secretaries, everyone refused to accept this offer as long as Murray was by the king's side. The outraged favourite declared that all the allegations against him were lies and slander, so he did not resign from his office. Eventually, the king convinced him to leave the court,[25] but this departure did not change much since his brother-in-law, John Hay, and his sister, Marjory, remained there.

The queen's position at the husband's royal court depended on the implementation of a few tasks which laid the foundation of their relationship. The failure of James Stuart's expedition in 1719 proved that Maria Clementina's connections were not sufficient enough for him to return to his heritage. The marriage took place, but the royal couple settled in Rome. It was only possible to hope that the relationship would bear fruit in the future and his wife's kinsmen would come to Stuart's assistance.

Another element in favour of marriage with Sobieska was the legendary wealth of her grandfather. Meanwhile, troubles with the payment of dowry, for which James Stuart waited for years, had to diminish the queen's position. The king's efforts[26] and Maria Clementina's timid requests[27] fill pages of many letters addressed to her father Prince James, but neither explanations nor the money arrived. Stuart's and Sobieski's men corresponded, made efforts and traveled to change the situation,[28] but according to the preserved sources, only a small part of the money reached James Stuart, and it was only before the queen's death.[29]

Maria Clementina managed to meet another obligation resting on the each queen. Already in November 1719, news about her pregnancy started to circulate.[30] It was probably fake news as the queen most likely suffered from the menstrual disorder, perhaps caused by anxiety – meeting her husband, expectations that she fulfills her duty and gives him a successor. She could also become pregnant and not notice

---

25 Corp 2011, p. 137–140.

26 James Stuart to James Sobieski, Montefiascone, 24 IX 1719, NGAB f. 694, o. 12, ms 268, ff. 17r–18v; James Stuart to James Sobieski, Albano, 14 VI 1723, NGAB f. 694, o. 12, ms 268, f. 72r-v.

27 Maria Clementina to James Sobieski, Montefiascone, 26 IX 1719, NGAB f. 694, o. 12, ms 358, cf 90r-v; Maria Clementina to James Sobieski, Rome, 26 I 1723, NGAB f. 694, o. 12, ms 360, f. 107r-v.

28 Jan Józef Spebach to James Sobieski, Paris, 5 XII 1719, NGAB f. 694, o. 12, ms 324, f. 1r-2v; Jan Józef Spebach to James Sobieski, Paris, 30 XI 1719, NGAB f. 694, o. 12, ms 324, f. 3r-4v; Michel Chateaudoux to NN, Rome, 11 XI 1719, NGAB f. 694, o. 12, ms 322, ff. 6r-7v; James Stuart and Maria Clementina to Daniel O'Brien, Rome,7 I 1733, RA SP Main/158, ff. 95–96.

29 James Sobieski's diploma, Żółkiew, 20 II 1733, Lvov 7 III 1733, RA SP Main/159, ff. 140–140b; James Sobieski's diploma, Oława, 13 VII 1733 RA SP Main/162, ff. 37–38.

30 Maria Clementina to James Sobieski, Rome, 17 XI 1719, NGAB f. 694, o. 12, ms 358, ff. 99r–100v.

the miscarriage.[31] At the beginning of 1720, James Stuart confirmed his wife's condition, but in fact she must have conceived in spring this year.[32] Waiting for the first childbirth must have been difficult. It is unknown whether women from Maria Clementina's circles could comfort and cheer her up if they were silent or kept telling some horrible stories. Hedwig Elisabeth barely survived her last childbirth in 1711; Maria Clementina must have remembered it and thus probably anxiously awaited for giving birth. Meanwhile, there was no lady by Maria Clementina's side who could state if the queen was pregnant and help her in childbirth. Countess Nithsdale, who had children, did not show up at the royal court, and Marjorie Hay was never pregnant and, being terrified, informed her husband that the queen was getting fatter and must have been afraid of childbirth. Lady Hay feared that, while having no experience herself, she would have to help Maria Clementina. There was also Eleanor Misset and a wet nurse, Lois Hughes, but among the ladies of high society, only Princess of Piombino – who belonged to the Roman society and on whom the duties associated with Sobieska's childbirth did not rest – could show up.[33]

Therefore, no one was taking care of the queen and her difficult situation. In contrast, when her grandmother, Marie Casimire, was expecting children from her first marriage to John Zamoyski, she went to the capital, to the court of her guardian, Queen Louise-Marie, in order to give birth under the care of the best physicians. Her first childbirths were difficult. When Hedwig Elisabeth got pregnant, Marie Casimire – already a queen at that time – acted accordingly, worrying about her daughter-in-law and trying to provide her possibly the safest childbirth. She invited her to come over, under the care of the court's doctors and many experienced ladies. Ladies from the major senatorial families were watching over the bed with Hedwig Elisabeth in childbirth. Taking care of the future mother and concern for their comfort – physical and mental – was the rule of conduct among the elites, but Maria Clementina was not taken care of that much, even though her child was to be the longed-for heir to the throne.

Charles Edward, Prince of Wales, was born on the 31st of December 1720 in the presence of the Roman elites and many cardinals. Rivalry over custody of him started immediately. James Stuart did not appoint a governess whom – due to her social rank – disliked Countess Nithsdale should have become, and Maria Clementina took over the supervision of her son's apartment. The position of the governess to the future ruler was desired since it gave aggrandisement in the royal court ladder, and it could provide the woman holding this function with

---

31 Michel Chateaudoux to NN, Rome, 23 XII 1719, NGAB f. 694, o. 12, ms 322, ff. 11r–12v.

32 James Stuart to James Sobieski, Rome, 27 I 1720, NGAB f. 694, o. 12, ms 268, f. 22r-v; James Stuart to James Sobieski, Rome, 12 IV 1720, NGAB f. 694, o. 12, ms 268, f. 28r-v.

33 Corp 2011, pp. 140,141.

an influence over the charge's upbringing. The Prince of Wales was given a wet nurse, nursemaids, chambermaids, and maidservants, and at the queen's request, Eleanor Misset became a sub-governess, but without a title due to her low social status. Other ladies appointed by the king and associated with the Jacobite circles in Saint-Germain-en-Laye refused to come to Rome on the grounds of their poor health. Misset enjoyed Sobieska's trust, but since she was taking care of the prince, she did not come to the queen's rooms. Apart from chambermaids and servants, the only woman who was there now was Marjorie Hay.[34]

Seemingly due to John Hay's pressure, the king soon removed Eleanor Misset from the prince's apartment without consulting this with his wife, which Maria Clementina did not like, especially since Misset also complained about the changes in her position. Perhaps she assumed she should obey only to the queen, which undermined James Stuart's rights and even more – his pride. In the background of these conflicts, Sobieska's dislike of Marjorie Hay was evident, and the latter – in her own opinion – also did not hold a favourable position and did not have any influence over the queen, for which she had hoped.

Soon the situation changed and Dorothy Sheldon, related to Arthur Dillon, came from France to Rome. She was recommended to the king by John Erskine, Duke of Mar, who was reluctant to Murray's and Hay's influences.[35] Sheldon made friends with the daughters of David Nairne, and she became part of Maria Clementina's circle of confidants who exchanged comments about the queen's difficult situation and the ill-treatment she received from the king's favourites.[36] The Prince of Wales' new guardian was well-informed on the Jacobites' politics, she also knew the late Queen Mary Beatrice, and she was aware of her influence. The arrival of Dorothy Sheldon brought further changes; the king ordered Eleanor Misset and Charles Wogan to leave Rome. This caused Maria Clementina's sorrow since she could have assumed that Misset – freed from her duties to the Prince of Wales – would return to her apartment. The queen's disappointment, who was still forced to the company of Marjorie Hay, and her caring for Charles Edward brought her closer to Dorothy Sheldon, and thus the queen remained in the circle of influence of the French Jacobites. According to the Duke of Mar, the change in the nursery was intended to impose a closer relationship with Lady Hay on Maria Clementina, but the matters had gone too far for the two women to change their connection. The queen – most likely stubborn and inclined to fight for her rights – was the more against the lady, the more she felt doomed to her company. It can be assumed that the queen who was emotional in her reactions but also in building relationships with people, did

---

34 Corp 2011, pp. 134, 141.

35 McLynn 2003, p. 136.

36 Corp 2018, pp. 391–392, 399.

not know how to pretend, and there were no reasons to give Lady Hay a second chance. It is also doubtful that the lady who was self-confident and confident about her position did not care of winning over Maria Clementina's sympathy.[37]

The situation in the nursery did not go according to the royal favourites' plans, but the greed for power and certainty about James Stuart's support made John Hay accuse Maria Clementina of yielding to emotions or even that she was not educated well enough. This accusation reappeared during the marital arguments.[38] Perhaps this objection was related toMaria Clementina's unwillingness to comply with her husband's decisions. Hay deemed that the queen was driven by the lust for power and warned the king that fulfilling the queen's expectations would be his undoing since it was him – as the king – who had to run his own household, and giving into female whims would mean a farewell not only to the royal power, but also the possibility to getting the throne back.[39] James Stuart – touchy, insecure, thirsty for support and stuck in a naive conviction of his own independence – succumbed to his favourite.[40]

The queen and her husband came from different cultural circles and had various life experiences. In Poland women held a strong position, replacing their husbands in the management of households in their absence; they usually enjoyed the freedom of making decisions about the family and its future. This was the experience of all Maria Clementina's Polish female ancestors, and she must have heard about the achievements of many of them. Her grandmother, Marie Casimire, a French woman brought up in Poland, was in vain trying to participate in the supervision of the property in her marriage to John Zamoyski, which he himself – busy with entertainments – did not look after; depriving her of this option and keeping her away from economic matters gave rise to her objection and this became one of the reasons for the breakdown of their relationship.[41] Maria Clementina most certainly knew about the influence Marie Casimire enjoyed later, not only within the family as the wife of John Sobieski but also as the queen.[42] Also, Maria Clementina's mother, Hedwig Elisabeth, and the latter's sister, Empress Eleonore, had a significant impact on the life of the Sobieski family. Almost everything that was taking place in their family in the beginning of the 18th century was the effect of their activities and

---

37 Corp 2011, p. 144.

38 Maria Clementina to James Sobieski, St. Cecilia convent, 2 II 1726, NGAB, f. 694. o. 12, ms 360, ff. 188r–189v.

39 Corp 2011, pp. 142–144

40 Porcelli 1949 = Ernest Porcelli, *The White Cockade. The Lives and Adventures of James Francis Edward Stuart and his Sons "Bonnie Prince Charlie" and Cardinal York*, London-New York-Melbourne-Sydney-Cape Town 1949, pp. 31–32.

41 Skrzypietz 2014, pp. 28–31.

42 Komaszyński 1983, pp. 131–164.

agreement in acting. Maria Clementina's father and uncles tried to run political activity, but when they were failing – what occurred often – these women saved them. The marriage of James and Hedwig Elisabeth took place thanks to Marie Casimire and Eleonore; life in Oława ran its course due to the empress' help.[43] Meanwhile, the position of women in Great Britain was relatively low, so the thought of listening to their advice or following them was unforgivable. A lot of Stuart queens – Anne of Denmark, Henrietta Maria, or Mary Beatrice, were accused of having a disastrous effect on their husbands.[44] James Stuart was brought up under the watchful eye of the energetic mother, and the thought of giving in to a woman was most certainly filling him with fear.[45] Moreover, his father also advised him to choose his wife very carefully.[46]

John Hay's manipulation that he used for his own purposes and threatening the king with Maria Clementina's influence was strengthening the favourite's position, at the same time destroying James Stuart's family life, but brought no political success. While the chances for winning back the throne were decreasing, James Stuart was increasingly more dependent on "the worse influences in his circles."[47] Furthermore, the financial issue must have also appeared in the background since the queen's dowry had still not been paid. John Hay's concerns regarding the queen's influence were all the more serious as he was aware of the support she enjoyed in France and at the Roman court. These divisions among the Jacobites cast a shadow on the relationship of the royal couple.

Tension at the royal court escalated in 1722. The Atterbury plot was set up in England; it was the most serious attempt to restore the House of Stuart to the throne since 1715.[48] The king was to secretly travel to Britain, and it was decided that his departure would be concealed by sending Maria Clementina to a health resort in Lucca. Her departure was considered sudden and unannounced, and many historians assumed it was the first sign of her later "madness".[49] Meanwhile, Edward Corp had proven that the purpose of the queen's travel was to explain James Stuart's sudden departure from Rome; officially, the king was to worry about the wife's absence and her health condition, and in reality, he was to leave for the British Isles. The plot failed, and after several weeks of travelling around Italy, the royal

43 Skrzypietz 2015, pp. 278–279, 284, 293, 306, 308.

44 Oman 1976, pp. 106–157; Oman 1962, p. 117,

45 Bevan 1962, pp. 39, 62.

46 Douglas 1998, p. 22.

47 Porcelli 1949, p. 36.

48 Cruishanks 2000, p. 243.

49 Niemojowska 1992, p. 139.

couple returned to Rome.[50] The queen's mother, Hedwig Elisabeth, died in August, so there were many reasons for sadness and disappointment.

In the same moment the Duke of Mar advised John Hay to send his wife away from court since rumours circulated that the queen did not like her, according to some people, because of her affair with the king. Out of the excessive impudence and self-confidence, or thoughtlessness, Hay – against all the rules – turned to Maria Clementina, most likely hoping that the queen would keep Marjorie at the court if she did not doubt the king's faithfulness. At that time, the king's adultery was neither reprehensible nor condemned. The monarch expressed in this way his physical strength and virility, and the mistress was becoming a broker of power, an intermediary in the access to the king's ear. However, this kind of situation in front of the Pope and in view of the financial support of the curia, and – which should not be doubted – James Stuart's innocence, would be unfortunate. Hay informed the queen that the rumour attributing jealously of Marjorie to her was undermining his and the king's honour. It is interesting that the monarch was mentioned as second. Hay argued that he had felt the queen's jealously already after the wedding but did not react, being certain of the faithfulness of the king and his own wife who would not have sacrificed her honour for any monarch. He asked Maria Clementina not to show this letter to the king, and particularly – to other women;[51] he most likely referred to those who were unfriendly towards Marjorie. The comment about Lady Hay who would not sacrifice her honour even for the ruler sounded exceptionally arrogant since it was not customary to refuse the monarch, and the thought of benefits and hopes for influence was more precious than keeping a lady's virtue of her husband's honour, who usually did not mind it since he could also benefit from it, and in case he objected, he could be sent away from court. Therefore, Hay's words were unbelievably brazen.

After a conversation with her husband, which she had had, the queen showed forgiveness and decided that Marjorie Hay could stay at the court.[52] It seems that by listening to the husband's pleas and by treating the Hays with grace, Maria Clementina made a mistake. She was considered weak, and the king's favourite and his wife strengthened their position. It is possible that the later events and the queen's sudden protest were all the most surprising for everyone.

As the result of these events, the Hays grew in strength and pride. Admittedly, John Hay lost his position as a *maggiordomo*, but the couple was moved to different rooms, which gave them both direct access to the king's and Charles Edward's apartments. Lady Hay was no longer in service to the queen, but John Hay started

50 Corp 2011, pp. 22–24.

51 John Hay to Maria Clementina, [n.p., n.d.] Thursday evening, RA SP Main/64, ff. 93–94.

52 Corp 2011, p. 147.

to suggest to Stuart that Maria Clementina's behaviour were whims associated with excessive expectations. The queen was to show discontentment because she had not received a separate court and her rightful position. It was this demand - of being independent in managing her own, although modest but separate, household - that was supposed to be a motive behind her actions. But it was the king who wanted to be the sole master of the court and family; moreover, he allegedly had no money to arrange a separate court for his wife.[53] No one noticed or did not want to notice, that the separate queen's court did not mean the monarch's loss of control over his wife's life and activities, and thus, giving into Maria Clementina's hands the decisions regarding the shape and composition of her circles would not go against her husband's position. The argument that the queen could not have her own court due to her husband's low income was disproved by the subsequent events. Moreover, Maria Clementina's revelations suggest that it was not her desire to control people at the court but to improve the relationship with her husband.[54]

John Hay's presence and his influence on the king was irritating not only to Maria Clementina. At the time, James Stuart was personally in charge of his correspondence since he had to do without the secretary of state. No one was ready to take over this honorific function as long as Hay remained at the court and misunderstandings in the Jacobite circles in exile were escalating. During the attempts to destroy any competition to the favours of the increasingly weaker monarch, arguments were not selected among the mutual accusations. The Duke of Mar, influential among the Jacobites, was accused of betraying the Atterbury plot; in turn, he replied that John Hay was speaking badly about the queen, forgetting that she was the wife of the king .[55]

Events of 1722 cast a shadow on the royal couple relationship. Maria Clementina was distancing herself from her husband, who was dependent on his favourites. Misunderstandings were increasing; the queen was locking herself in the rooms, seeing no one apart from her chambermaids and valets. In July 1723, Countess Nithsdale did not receive permission to see the queen.[56] This voluntary isolation was an expression of Maria Clementina's protest. She clearly wanted to get her husband's attention, but she did not manage to draw his interest. Busy with his correspondence, the aim of which - maintaining the Jacobites' interest - was becoming increasingly more illusory, the king had no time for his wife.He believed that political affairs could not be the topic for discussions and considerations with the queen, but he entrusted them to his favourites, which irritated Sobieska.

---

53 Corp 2011, 147–148.

54 Maria Clementina Sobieska to James Stuart, from the house in Rome, 10 XI 1725, NGAB, f. 694. o. 12, ms 360, f. 196r–196v.

55 Corp 2011, pp. 149,151–152.

56 Ibidem, p. 149.

It must be emphasized that from the beginning of her marriage and despite the increasing tensions, Maria Clementina never avoided public celebrations, balls, and musical events. The royal couple's presence graced religious ceremonies, and Sobieska fulfilled her representative and social duties with great charm and – to a certain moment – with commitment.[57]

A breakaway between Maria Clementina and Stuart took place in 1725; after the birth of the second son, Henry Benedict, the king decided that Charles Edward would come under the authority of men. This happened prematurely because the prince was only four years old. The king did not discuss this decision with Maria Clementina, and he wanted to give the son to James Murray. Dorothy Sheldon openly spoke against the king; her behaviour confirms James Stuart's weak position, but this was not the end of quarrels. In November, Murray forbade the queen to visit the Prince of Wales and to leave her alone with her son; he was allegedly acting on the king's orders. As a consequence, Maria Clementina made a scene and then, in protest, left the palace and moved to the convent of Saint Cecilia in Trastevere. This was the beginning of the spouses' separation, which lasted two years. To the great surprise of those around her, the queen not only opposed her husband but openly spoke against him, demanding the removal of his favourites from the court, and she achieved her goal. Not only her attitude but also the success she achieved was astonishing in view of her previous inclination, seemingly accepting the unrestrained governance of her husband's henchmen. The support she was given and the high price for her success is beyond the scope of this article, but the story she told her father about it in her correspondence is an interesting image of a woman fighting for her rights.[58]

The first six years that Maria Clementina spent in Rome were a time of happiness when she met her husband after months of waiting for their meeting, when their sons were born, and when she delighted the Roman circles with her grace and sensitivity. However, it turned out that their relationship was not free from problems, Sobieska's connections did not help James Stuart to win back his throne, and the fabulous dowry was an empty promise. Like many other queens, Maria Clementina became the target of struggles between factions that were shaking the court and Jacobite emigrants. It is not clear how consciously she joined this game. While seeking her husband's understanding and attention, she opposed his favourites, who depreciated her position and tried to deprive her of influence on the court. When the fight reached the children's nursery and James Murray – pleading the monarch's order – did not allow the queen to see her son, her previous calmness and

---

57 "Gazette de France", Rome, 2 X 1722, 21 XI 1722, 13 II 1723, 3 VII 1723, 17 VII 1723, 31 VII 1723, 23 IX 1724, 21 X 1724, 18 XI 1724, 25 XI 1724, 30 XII 1724.

58 A. Skrzypietz, *Maria Clementina Sobieska and Her Efforts to Win Her Husband's Respect and Own Independence* (forthcoming).

assumed acceptance of her own weakness turned into anger; she took up the fight for her position, access to children and husband with conviction and determination.

Bibliography

Archive sources

AGAD AR =Archiwum Główne Akt Dawnych Archiwum Radziwiłłów II, Warsaw, ms 2387.

NGAB = Nacyjanlnyj Gistarycznyj Archiu Biełarusi, Minsk, fond 694, opis 12, ms 268, 322, 324, 350, 358, 359, 360.

RA SP = Royal Archives Stuarts Papers, London, Main/32, 43, 44, 64, 158,159, 162

Printed sources

Wogan 1894 = Charles Wogan, *Mémoires sur l'enterprise d'Inspruck en 1719. Dedicated to the Queen of France*. In: *Narratives of the Detention, Liberation and Marriage of Maria Clementina Stuart Styled Queen of Great Britain and Ireland with Contemporary Letters and Papers Now for the First Time Published*. Ed. By John T. Gilbert, Dublin 1894.

"Gazette de France"

Modern sources

Bevan 1962 = Bryan Bevan, *King James the Thrid of England: A Study in Kingship*, Robert Hayle, London 1962.

Corp 2011 = Edward Corp, *The Stuarts in Italy, 1719-1766. A Royal Court in Permament Exile*, University Press, Cambridge 2011.

Corp 2018 = Edward Corp, *Sir David Nairne. The Life of a Scottish Jacobite at the Court of The Exiled* Stuarts. Studies in the History and Culture of Scotland, nr 8, Peter Lang Publishing, Oxford–Bern–Berlin–Brussels–Frankfurt on the Main–New York–Vienna 2018.

Cruishanks 2000 = Eveline Cruickshanks, *The Duke of Ormonde and the Atterbury Plot*. In: *The Dukes of Ormonde, 1610–1745*, ed. Toby Barnard Jane Fenlon, Boydell Press, Wolbridge 2000.

Daiches 1973 = David Daiches, *Charles Edward Stuart. The Life and Times of Bonnie Prince Charlie*, Pan Books, London 1973.

Douglas 1998 = Hugh Douglas, *The Private Passions of Bonnie Prince Charlie*, Stroud, Sutton 1998.

Gürtler 1991 = Gernot O. Gürtler, *Kalkulacja polityczna czy racja stanu? Kulisy pobytu w Innsbrucku wnuczki Jana III Sobieskiego*, trans. by Magdalena Chudzicka, Jerzy Fudalej, Urszula Świtka, Agencja Dziennikarska „Vipress". Lublin 1991.

Komaszyński 1983 = Michał Komaszyński, *Maria Kazimiera d'Arquien Sobieska królowa Polski (1641–1716)*, Wydawnictwo Literackie, Cracow 1983.

McLynn 2003 = Frank McLynn, *Bonnie Prince Charlie*, Pimilco, London 2003.

Miller 1968 = Peggy Miller, *Żona dla Pretendenta, rzecz o Marii Klementynie Sobieskiej*, trans. Anna Przedpełska-Trzeciakowska, „Czytelnik", Warsaw 1968.

Niemojowska 1992 = Maria Niemojowska, *Ostatni Stuartowie*, PIW, Warsaw 1992.

Oman 1976 = Carola Oman, *Henrietta Maria*, White Lion Publishers Ltd., London-Sydney-Toronto 1976.

Oman 1962 = Carola Oman, *Mary of Modena*, Hodder & Stoughton, London 1962.

Porcelli 1949 = Ernest Porcelli, *The White Cockade. The Lives and Adventures of James Francis Edward Stuart and his Sons "Bonnie Prince Charlie" and Cardinal York*, Hutchinson, London 1949.

Shield, Lang 1907 = Alice Shield, Andrew Lang: *The King* over the Water, Longmans & Co, London 1907.

Skrzypietz = Aleksandra Skrzypietz, *Maria Clementina Sobieska and Her Efforts to Win Her Husband's Respect and Own Independence* (forthcoming).

Skrzypietz 2014 = Aleksandra Skrzypietz, *Rozkwit i upadek rodu Sobieskich*, „Bellona", Warsaw 2014.

Skrzypietz 2015 = *Jakub Sobieski*, Wydawnictwo Poznańskie, Poznań 2015.

Szajnocha 1909 = Karol Szajnocha, *Wnuka króla Jana* III, in: Karol Szajnocha, *Szkice historyczne*, Józef Unger, Warsaw 1909.

Katarzyna Kuras

Networking Traps. Marie Leszczyńska in the Polish and French Dynastic Arrangements*

Abstract:

Marie Leszczyńska, the daughter of King Stanisław I of Poland, and the wife of the French monarch, Louis XV, lived in various dynastic and courtly worlds. Changes of these worlds took place in extraordinary circumstances which determined the course of her life and position. The election of Stanisław Leszczyński as the king in 1704 meant for this noblewoman from Greater Poland that she received a princess status, while the marriage to the King of France in 1725 equated to taking an honourable place by the side of the monarch of one of the most important states on the map of Europe.

The key to understanding the "traps of the net", in which Leszczyńska found herself as a result of these changes, is the analysis of the position and functioning of the Polish princess and French queen in the different worlds of dynastic and personal dependencies. It is of particular importance to juxtapose and compare the structures of networks to which Leszczyńska belonged, their range, prestige, and the existing interactions and influences. It seems that the weak position of Louis XV's wife in Versailles stemmed not only from the lack of any support by the local palace factions but also from a relatively low level of participation in the European community of rulers by the Leszczyński family. The aim of this article is to analyse these relations and to determine their influence on Marie Leszczyńska's life course, as well as the position she held both in Poland and France.

On the 18th of December 1725, Queen Marie Leszczyńska was in tears. Married a few months earlier to the King of France, Louis XV, she most likely did not expect that her happiness by her husband's side would be so short. On this unfortunate day, she agreed to take part in an intrigue which had been planned by her protector and – as it seemed – her only friend at the French royal court, Prince Louis-Henri de Bourbon-Condé. Throughout the king's minority, the prince was the head of the Regency Council, and then he took the office of the first minister. He was the one responsible for sending Louis' fiancée, Mariana Victoria, back to Madrid and

* The research conducted to prepare this article was part of the project 2014/13/B/HS3/04975 « The Court of Queen Marie Leszczyńska. Its People, Money and Influence » financed by the National Science Centre, Poland.

for selecting the daughter of the former King of Poland, Stanisław I Leszczyński, to become his wife. All these actions were supported by an influential mistress, Jeanne Agnès de Pléneuf, Marquise de Prie. The prince did realise that his position by Louis XV's side was not unchallenged. Cardinal André-Hercule de Fleury, the monarch's tutor and mentor, also enjoyed the ruler's great trust. 1725 brought quite a lot of uncertainty regarding the power balance between the first minister and the cardinal; the former was clearly losing his position in the structures of power and at the royal court. The game he had undertaken in order to strengthen his significance was aimed at discrediting the cardinal in the eyes of the monarch and at removing him from having impact on the French politics. To achieve this goal, the prince decided to use the young queen's intermediation. He probably did not have to convince her for a long time to agree to arrange a meeting with Louis XV in her chambers. The prince hoped that the unofficial conversation with the king would let him win back his complete trust and stabilise his position as the first minister. This strategy turned out to be thoroughly ineffective. The king – unaware of anything – decided that he had been put by his wife in a greatly awkward situation; he was also most sceptical towards the information on the cardinal. As a result of these events, Prince de Bourbon-Condé lost Louis XV's trust, and he was removed from the royal court a few months later (Marquise de Prie met a similar fate). On the very same day – the 18th of December – the king summoned his preceptor to return from Issy, where he had taken refuge, awaiting the outcome of events.[1]

In December 1725, the queen allowed to be drawn into a game that exceeded her skills to act and the knowledge on the palace networks. The king convinced her to humble herself to Cardinal de Fleury. From then on, the mutual relations between Leszczyńska and the cardinal were marked by a far-reaching aloofness, with the queen having the dominant feeling of powerlessness in the relations with the omnipresent clergyman. After Prince de Bourbon-Condé was sent away, the queen was certain that she had been treated instrumentally and additionally she had been discredited in the monarch's eyes. Duchess de Carignan noted that the queen – deprived of the prince's protection – was behaving like a lost child.[2] At the same time, this was the cardinal's masterful move which within one December afternoon eliminated every opponent aspiring to have an influence on Louis XV. The king did not trust his wife any longer, and the first minister was removed. Therefore, the cardinal had no more competitors.

The queen's biographers are keen to return to the situation from the 18th of December 1725 because they see it as the reason for the weak position that Louis

1 Campbell 1996, 97–99.

2 Rogister 2004, 200.

XV's spouse held in the official and unofficial power structures.[3] Unsuccessful intervention in favour of Prince de Bourbon-Condé was her only individual attempt at wielding some influence on the network of the court's factions. For the next 43 years spent by Louis XV's side, the queen did not repeat the mistake from the beginning of her marriage. Admittedly, rumours appeared in the 1750s and 1760s that she belonged to a group of leaders of the so-called pious coterie, but there is no indication that Leszczyńska played a particularly significant role within this formation.[4] Her characteristic apoliticism clearly fit into the role traditionally ascribed to a ruler's spouse. First and foremost, she was meant to be his life companion and a mother of royal children, at the same time not aspiring to play any specific role in France. On the other hand, the king's wife was a potential regent, and due to her natural closeness to the monarch, she was predestined to participate in the unofficial mechanisms of power. Her function also enjoyed considerable prestige, from which the previous queens were able to benefit to some extent.[5]

Leszczyńska's weak position and her slim influence associated with it were rather obvious for her contemporaries and historians who – apart from reaching for the events from December of 1725 – tried to search for other reasons of the queen's passivity. While creating an apologetic vision of her life, Abbé Proyart claimed that she had not gotten involved with politics because of being driven solely by moral motives.[6] Benedetta Craveri, who tried to present Leszczyńska against the background of earlier queens, emphasised her commitment to family life and devotion to her own passions.[7] While explaining the attitude of Louis XV's wife, the focus was either on the lack of her aspirations to play an important role at the royal court or the fact that she was placed against the background of a peculiar arrangement dominating from the 1740s, in which the king trusted the cardinal first, then his mistress, and the royal spouse was consciously pushed away by him from influence on making any decisions.

All these explanations seem to be rather convincing in the context of the dynastic reality of the 18th century. The territory of predominantly monarchical Europe was covered in a thick net of family arrangements and dependencies, steered by rulers and members of their families. In order to preserve power and *status quo*, they cooperated together and, while using the rules of succession and marriage, they decided about the exclusive nature of this group. The French historian, Lucien Bély, wrote about the society of princes (*la société des princes*), which he defined as a group consisting of those how ruled, their families and relatives, linked together

3 Muratori-Philip 2010, 77–79.

4 Hours 2006, 16–18.

5 Cosandey 2000.

6 Proyart 1825, 109–110.

7 Craveri 2007, 241–251.

with various – ideological, political, economic, and family – means.[8] Andreas Kraus, who analysed the connections and position of the Wittelsbachs, noticed that one could get an impression that until the end of the *ancien régime*, Europe was ruled by one huge family, divided into smaller lines.[9] Although this opinion seems to be slightly exaggerated, the very existence of the European networks of rulers is not in doubt. It was based on blood ties, additionally strengthened by marriages within the dynasties of those in power (sometimes within a very limited circle).[10] Its members shared the sense of belonging to the elitist community that was rather conservative in its views. These characteristics, together with the strong economic position that was the heritage of the Middle Ages, guaranteed that individual dynasties and the entire network would last.[11] Its solidity and durability were ensured by women. It was a standard in dynastic Europe to have marriages between the representatives of families in power, which were scrupulously negotiated when the future spouses were still children and concluded in accordance with the existing political alliances.[12] This was particularly important in the conditions of the primogeniture rule, which was gaining popularity with regard to inheritance and succession.[13]

From women's point of view, belonging to the dynastic network was beneficial. It gave them family and diplomatic support, particularly when they left their native court and went to their husbands' residences. Being deprived of this kind of support could have resulted in various perturbations, which were experienced i.e. by Anne of Austria, who was temporarily at the mercy of Louis XIII and Cardinal de Richelieu. The community of rulers was such an elitist and closed off circle that the instances of getting into it by any other way than birth or marriage were sporadic. The aim of this article is to present the history of a princess who reached the top of the dynastic network through "the back door". Marie Leszczyńska's position in the palace networks of Versailles can be explained through the perspective of her preferences or personality, but the Polish and French dynastic arrangements, in which she had to function, seem to be much more important. For this reason, the article will present the meanders of the Polish position of the Leszczyński family (until 1725) and two Bourbons, whom Marie came across quite unexpectedly. In order to explain the place of Louis XV's spouse in a complex dynastic network, it is necessary to juxtapose and compare the structures to which Leszczyńska belonged, their scope, prestige, the existing interactions and influences.

---

8 Bély 1999.

9 Kraus 1981, 426.

10 Tischer 2008, 39–53; Kohler 1994, 461–482.

11 Schönpflug 2010.

12 Morton, Watanabe-O'Kelly 2016.

13 Hohkamp 2007, 91–104.

Poland in Dynastic Arrangements

The elective throne of Poland created a set of complication in the functioning of the monarch and their families in the dynastic arrangements. These complications became particularly clear throughout the reigns of "kings-compatriots" – Michał Korybut Wiśniowiecki and John III Sobieski. Both rulers made some effort, quite successful at that, to establish themselves in the then community of rulers – Michał Korybut married a representative of the Habsburg family and John III made sure that his son James married the daughter of the Rhine Elector Palatine Hedwig Elisabeth of Palatinate-Neuburg, and the daughter Theresa Kunegunda was married off to the Elector of Bavaria, Maximilian II Emanuel. Augustus II the Strong was also in a privileged position since, as the Elector of Saxony, he had a number of connections, primarily in the territories of the Reich. In comparison to him, the situation of King Stanisław Leszczyński, elected in 1704, was highly unfavourable. He was a nobleman from Greater Poland and, therefore, no serious dynastic arrangements supported him. Additionally, his election took place in the conditions allowing it to put its legality in doubt. Leszczyński's election was decided by the King of Sweden, Charles XII Wittelsbach, who was running a military campaign against Russia and Saxony – as part of the Great Northern War – in the territories of the Kingdom of Poland. He needed Stanisław Leszczyński as a puppet, which was a counterweight to Augustus II the Strong. The election was arranged in 1704 in Warsaw, and its participants were aware that the Swedish army of Arvid Horn was stationed nearby. Leszczyński's proclamation was not done, in accordance with tradition, by Primate Mikołaj Radziejowski, but by the Bishop of Poznań, Mikołaj Święcicki, and the coronation of the new ruler did not take place, as the ritual dictated, in Cracow controlled by the Saxons, but in Warsaw. Even new regalia were used during the coronation because the old insignia were removed from the treasury in Wawel on Augustus II's order.[14]

Therefore, Leszczyński's position as the king was questionable, and, in addition, he was financially dependent on his patron after the Saxon army had taken over his family estates. In order to maintain his position, the king was forced to constant and humiliating negotiations with Charles XII, during which he wrote i.e.: "I sacrificed myself for maintaining the glory of His Majesty, this obliges me to tell you honestly that I have no means of support."[15] All the weaknesses of the procedure, during which Leszczyński had been elected, as well as his actual dependence on Charles XII, were skillfully used by political opponents who held the position of recognising the legality of Augustus II's power. Handwritten copies of documents circulated

---

14 Cieślak 1994, 40–56.

15 Cieślak 1994, 49.

around the country, including public letters, manifestos and lampoons, in which Leszczyński's election and kingship were questioned.[16] King Stanisław replied to his opponents and ran an intensive campaign using various arguments, but this did not affect his actual position.[17]

Dynastic arrangements of Stanisław Leszczyński depended exclusively on Charles XII. The Polish king was dependent not only on the Swedish army but also on the Swedish connections. The influences of the Rhine Wittelsbach, who originated from the County Palatine of Zweibrücken and ruled Sweden, were limited to northern Europe and the Reich, where the family was in charge of some territories.[18] The Wittelsbachs were Lutherans, and they selected their spouses from a limited religious circle.[19] Charles XII's mother was a Danish princess, Ulrika Eleonora, and his grandmother was Princess Hedwig Eleonora of Holstein-Gottorp (she was chosen as a wife for Charles X Gustav by Queen Kristina). Holstein was a traditional point of support in the politics against Denmark – in 1698, Hedvig Sophia, the elder sister of Charles XII, married the local duke (and also her cousin), Frederick IV.[20] In turn, the Rhine Wittelsbachs, who married within the Reich, cemented their connections to the local dynasties, including Baden-Durlach, Nassau-Saarbrücken, Brunswick-Lüneburg, Orange, and Veldenz. Hesse was also a strong point of support for Charles XII – the wife of the local prince, Frederick, was Ulrika Eleonora (the later queen), the sister of the Swedish king.[21]

Charles' connections within the Reich turned out to be exceptionally valuable for Leszczyński when after the battle of Poltava in 1708, he was deprived of actual help from the Swedish king. In 1714 Charles XII appointed King Stanisław a *duc par délégation* in the County Palatine of Zweibrücken. Leszczyński managed the County Palatine until February 1719. Together with the death of Charles XII, a serious reshuffling took place within the network in which he lived. Power in Sweden passed into the hands of Ulrika Eleonora while the County Palatine of Zweibrücken was inherited by Gustav Samuel Leopold, Count Palatine of Kleeburg, who originated from the dynasty's branch line.[22] The Polish king was in a difficult situation which

16 I.a. "Mother warns Stanisław Leszczyński about his enthronement", AGAD, Branicki Collections in Sucha 285/356, fol. 78v-79; "Rhythm about Stanisław, the King of Poland", BK, manuscript 513, fol. 127.

17 Porazinski 1999, 128–156, 193–194.

18 In 1615, the ruler of the County Palatine of Zweibrücken, John Casimir, married the daughter of Charles IX of Sweden, Catherine. Their son was Charles X Gustav of Sweden, the grandfather of Charles XII and the first of the Rhine Wittelsbachs on the Swedish throne. Kraus 1981, 434.

19 Morton, Watanabe-O'Kelly 2016, 233.

20 Details regarding the Lutheran network in Scandinavia and the northern Reich in: Neville, Skogh 2017, 4.

21 Hatton 1969.

22 Bély 1999, 376.

he tried to get out of by using the only arrangements available to him, i.e. those inherited from his acquaintance with Charles XII. The skills and consistency with which he organised his own financial help from the monarchs of Sweden, the duke of Lorraine, and the French regent, Philippe II, Duke of Orléans, allows suggesting that in the political reality of 1719, the noble origins of the king, as well as the awareness of circumstances in which he had been crowned, did not decide about his actual position among the rulers of Europe. A factor deciding about the status of the Polish king was the fact that he had once been under the protection of Charles XII, which equated to being included in the elitist dynastic network. When granting Leszczyński the permission to reside in Alsatian Landlau, Philippe II, Duke of Orléans wrote that "France has always been a refuge for miserable princes".[23]

Therefore, Leszczyński's powers should not be overestimated. Charles XII's position in the net. which was co-created with the Wittelsbachs and allies. was gradually weakening after the defeat at Poltava (the very network most likely also eroded to some extent).[24] In these arrangements, Leszczyński was probably a mere pawn whose actions were thoroughly dependent on his patron's will. After the death of the Swedish king, his existence was as obvious for the then rulers and diplomats as it was troubling. The dramatic situation of the Polish king was revealed in full during his stay in Wissembourg. The most acute symptom of the crisis were the efforts, which the king made in order to marry off his only living daughter, Marie, to someone who belonged to the then French or German elite. Initially, they relied on the Swedish diplomats who tried to match the princess with Margrave Louis-Georges von Baden-Baden. The reason for breaking off the negotiations was the lack of Marie's dowry. In this situation, there was a plan of her marriage to Louis-Charles-Cézar Le Tellier, Marquis of Courtenvaux. The candidature had some drawbacks. The marquis was indeed wealthy, and, additionally, he was the grandson of famous Louvois, but according to Leszczyński his rank was too low for the king's daughter! King Stanisław conditioned his consent to this marriage by elevating the candidate to the position of duke or peerage, which turned out to be impossible in the then political constellation. Failures in the efforts to gain a favourable marriage for Marie, together with the financial misery in which the Leszczyński family was forced to exist, were striking proof of the inferior position they actually had in the monarchic network. Marie's appearance on the Paris exchange of matrimonial names – initially as a candidate for the wife of the first minister Louis-Henri de Bourbon-Condé and then King Louis XV – did not stem from her beauty of social connections. It was probably the result of King Stanisław's social acquaintance with the Archbishop of Strasbourg, Cardinal Armand-Gaston-Maximilien de Rohan, a man who was

---

23 "La France a toujours été l'asile des rois malheureux". Voltaire 1878, 318.

24 Por. Granovetter 1973, 1360–1380.

very influential at the royal court (the cardinal held an honourable function of the royal almoner). There is no doubt that Princess Marie met rather confusing criteria, according to which the wife for Louis XV was being selected. She was healthy and older than the ruler, thus giving hope for a quick childbirth of the offspring, and, additionally, she was by no means linked to the French dynastic network or the royal court, which – in a highly complicated reality of 1725 – was, paradoxically, a powerful asset.[25]

French Dynastic Network

Events of 1725 and the surprising marriage of Louis XV triggered ambivalent opinions of the contemporaries and historians. Marquis d'Argenson, an astute observer, noted on this occasion that the new queen was chosen by the mistress of Prince of Bourbon-Condé, Marquise de Prie, and she had done this with such a nonchalance with which he would normally recruit valets.[26] On the other hand, the historians, i.e. Pierre Boyé and Emanuel Rostworowski, emphasised the potential this marriage offered to the international arena, leading to the recovery of Lorraine by France.[27] In 1725, this potential was very vague, and the queen – particularly after the 18th of December – was forced to manoeuvre in the royal court arrangements. This was very difficult from her point of view, particularly since she was devoid of any personal or dynastic support. In 1725 no one – neither on the Polish nor the French side – was particularly concerned about providing the princess with at least a substitute for her native retinue. No negotiations were undertaken in order to i.e. include one of the Polish aristocrats in the group of the palace's ladies-in-waiting. King Stanisław was sufficiently satisfied with the proposal of marriage from Versailles, and there is no indication he cared about such details as the setting of the future queen's *maison*. His opportunities to exert influence were hugely limited (if not none), hence Leszczyński decided to prepare only advice for his daughter, in which he offered his own vision of the French queen's role by the side of her husband and the ruler of the Kingdom.[28] The Versailles' decision-makers were rather keen on using the passive attitude which dominated the Polish party.

The Leszczyński family – so far levitating on the outskirts of the network consisting of the Wittelsbachs and their allies in the Reich – did not have much in common with the circles Queen Marie joined in 1725. The Bourbons belonged

25 Boyé 1933, 2–9, Raynal 1887. The circumstances between Louis XV and Marie Leszczyńska were described in detail in: Samsel 2007.

26 Argenson 1859, 60.

27 Boyé 1939; Rostworowski 1963, 9–65.

28 *Conseils du Roy de la Pologne à la Reine de France sa fille*, BPP, ms 92, fol. 1–11.

to the group of the most eminent European dynasties. They originated from the branch line of the Capetian dynasty; its founder, Robert de Clermont (died 1317), was the youngest son of Louis IX of France and Margaret of Provence. In 1589 after the end of the House of Valois, the first of the Bourbons, Henry IV, sat on the French throne. The dynastic network, in which the subsequent representatives of the dynasty moved, was limited to the Catholic cycle. Although the French rulers were following the state's rule of law in international affairs and they did not hesitate to form alliances with the protestant countries like Turkey, they did nevertheless use the religious key while creating the grounds for family politics. However, when they decided to make exceptions in this regard, like in the case of Charles I Stuart's wife, Henrietta Maria, it was on the condition that the queen remained a Catholic.[29] In the 17th century, the French Bourbons were willingly entering into marriages with the representatives of the Spanish Habsburgs. In 1612, Marie de'Medici and the Duke of Lerma negotiated a double wedding – King Louis was supposed to get married to Infanta Anna while his sister, Elisabeth, was to marry the ruler of Spain, Philip IV.[30] In 1660 a wedding between Louis XIV and Infanta Maria Theresa of Austria took place as part of the cementing of the peace concluded between France and Spain. Relationships with the Italian duchies were also popular. This tradition was initiated in the times of the Bourbons by Christine, the daughter of Henry IV and Marie de'Medici, who married the Duke of Savoy, Victor Amadeus I, in 1619 (in 1637–1648, she was even a regent of Savoy).[31] Family ties with the Italian duchies were maintained by Louis XIV. His grandsons – Louis and Philip – were married to princesses – and sisters at the same time – of Savoy, Marie Adélaïde and Maria Luisa. The monarch also maintained some traditional contacts with the duchies of the Reich. The second wife of his brother Philippe I, Duke of Orléans, was Elizabeth Charlotte, Madame Palatine from the Wittelsbach's dynasty. Before the wedding in 1671, she had to be publicly converted to Catholicism.[32] The wife of the only son of the Sun King, Louis, also known as the Grand Dauphin, was Maria Anna Victoria (*la Grande Dauphine*) of Bavaria. Even though this relationship was not the happiest one, it was proof that France and Bavaria operated within the same network of political and dynastic alliances.[33] As a result of the dynastic politics conducted with large momentum, the Bourbons were related to an extensive group of European dynasts. The networks they created were overlapped by links made as a

29 Henrietta Maria could not be crowned to the Queen of England; Catholicism did not do her any favours in England either. Smuts 2016, 13–36.

30 McGowan 2016.

31 Ferretti 2014, 7–20.

32 Van der Cruysse 2001, 139–140.

33 Hartmann 1981, 269–289. France, Bavaria and Savoy were connected in the 17th century by an intricate web of dynastic marriages: Nicklas 2009.

result of the politics of their contracting parties, resulting in Europe being covered in a dense mosaic of family dependencies. L. Bély meticulously counted that the great-grandson of Louis XIV and the grandson of the Grand Dauphin, Louis XV, was related to the houses ruling in Austria, Spain, Denmark, Sweden, Bavaria, and the Saxon dynasties (including the branch of Albertine Electorate), and a significant number of the Reich's state. He also had numerous uncles and cousins in Italy.[34]

It was difficult to get rid of the impression triggered by Leszczyńska's connections and viewed against this background. Granting Lorraine to King Stanisław in 1738 did not change much in this respect. Even the birth of the dauphin, Louis Ferdinand, in 1729 was rather stabilising than strengthening her position. Józef Aleksander Jabłonowski, present at the French court, noted at the time that "since the birth of the dauphin, the French queen began to rule the roost more",[35] but this opinion seems to be much exaggerated. When one year later, another son was born, Philippe of Anjou, the future of the dynasty seemed to be secured. However, this situation did not last for long since in 1733, the younger son of the royal couple died unexpectedly, and the queen was giving birth to girls only, to her husband's great disappointment.[36] The queen was invariably a potential regent, which was recalled usually at the times of the king's indispositions. In 1752, a purely hypothetical question was considered at the royal court on whether the queen – or the dauphine – would become a regent in the event of the king's death.[37] Leszczyńska's weak position in the dynastic networks was also evidenced by her lack of involvement in the matter of her children's marriages. Subsequent candidates for the dauphin's wife were chosen in accordance with the alliances of France; the queen was only unsuccessfully trying to torpedo the plans of her son's second marriage to Maria Josepha of the House of Wettin, the daughter of Augustus III of Poland. A Saxon diplomat, Johann Adolf von Loss, who was aware of the fact, who was really in charge of Versailles, noted at that time that the queen would "relent as always".[38] Von Loss was right – the queen not only yielded, but she also quickly conveyed her confidence and affection in the dauphine. Leszczyńska did not have many opportunities to prove herself in the marriage arrangements – out of eight daughters she gave birth to, only one, Louise Élisabeth, was married off. In 1739 she married the Duke of Parma, Philip, thus continuing the tradition of French-Italian relationships.

34 Bély 1999, 369–382.

35 LNB, f. 102, file 422, part 2, fol. 155–156, J.A. Jabłonowski to T. Jabłonowska, [Paris], 1754].

36 Nolhac 1900, 81–87.

37 Argenson 1859, 290, 313; Soulavie 1802, 283.

38 Wyleżyńska 1923, 136.

Conclusions

Tears that the queen shed on the evening of the 18th of December 1725 resulted not only from her disappointment in the situation and her humiliation, which she had suffered from Cardinal de Fleury. They were also the effect of a bitter understanding of her actual position at the French royal court. The already mentioned passivity of the queen throughout all these years she spent by Louis XV's side could have been the result of the experience she was getting this way, and not a deliberate choice – as was suggested by some of the biographers – since this was something Leszczyński's daughter most likely did not have. The analysis of the dynastic networks in which the Polish princess functioned, confirms this conclusion. The Polish network was very limited due to the specificity of the elective throne. Throughout the Great Northern War, Stanisław Leszczyński was "tied in" to the Swedish arrangements, which he skilfully used in various international games. However, the Swedish – protestant – network could not be a sufficient trampoline for an advantageous marriage of King Stanisław's only daughter. The daughter, who at the same time was his greatest capital. The interests of Warsaw, Stockholm, and Paris were very heterogeneous in terms of dynastic matters, and the only link between Stanisław – who drifted on the French-German frontier and held onto the Swedish royal court – and the policymakers in Paris was, in fact, Cardinal de Rohan. It was to him and his arrangements with Prince of Bourbon-Condé that Marie Leszczyńska owed her surprising marriage to Louis XV. It seems that despite an optimistic view of E. Rostworowski, the daughter of King Stanisław was in fact "a Cinderella" in a marriage puzzle of 1725 and a victim of the dynastic networking traps, in which she found herself due to various positions and connections of her father and her husband.

Therefore, it is not possible to regard Leszczyńska's place in the then dynastic arrangements as the only factor explaining the strategy she adopted at the French royal court. Even the queens and dauphines, whose families belonged to the circles close to Versailles, received limited support on that account. Maria Theresa of Austria, the wife of Louis XIV, who came from the Habsburg dynasty, did not have any influence on the royal court's affairs because that was the will of her husband, and Maria Anna Victoria, who represented the Wittelsbachs of Bavaria, was eliminated from the sphere of power due to the crisis of the French-Bavarian alliance and the illness. Thus, Marie Leszczyńska was not all alone in this company. Everything she gained in Versailles, she owed to her good upbringing, intellect, and an extraordinary skill to adapt to the world of the royal court. When her tears dried, the queen took on her role, which she performed reliably and with good sense for the next 43 years.[39]

Bibliography

Manuscript sources and unpublished works

AGAD = Archiwum Główne Akt Dawnych; The Central Archives of Historical Records, Zbiory Branickich z Suchej [Branicki Collections in Sucha] 285/356, f. 78v-79, "Matka przestrzega Stanisława Leszczyńskiego w intronizacyi jego".

BK = Biblioteka Kórnicka PAN; PAN Library in Kórnik, ms 513, fol. 127, "Rytm o Stanisławie królu polskim".

LNB = Vasyl Stefanyk National Scientific Library of Ukraine in Lviv, f. 102, file 422, part 2

BPP = Bibliothèque Polonaise, Paris, manuscript 92, fol. 1–11, *Conseils du Roy de la Pologne à la Reine de France sa fille.*

Printed sources

Argenson 1859 = *Journal et mémoires du marquis d'Argenson,* vol. I, éd. Edmé-Jacques-Benoît Rathery, Vve Jules Renouard, Paris 1859.

Soulavie 1802 = Jean-Louis Soulavie, *Mémoires historiques et anecdotes de la cour de France pendant la faveur de Marquise de Pompadour*, Arthus Bertrand, Paris 1802.

Voltaire 1878 = Voltaire, *Histoire de Charles XII*, Vol. 16. *Œuvres complètes de Voltaire,* Garnier, Paris 1878.

Modern sources

Bély 1999 = Lucien Bély, *La société des princes*, Fayard, Paris 1999.

Boyé 1933 = Pierre Boyé, *Autour du mariage de Marie Leszczynska*, in: *Quatre études inédites*, Lorraine Art Graphiques, Nancy 1933.

Boyé 1939 = Pierre Boyé, *Le mariage de Marie Leszczynska et l'Europe*, Éditions Berger-Levrault, Nancy-Paris-Strasbourg 1939.

Campbell 1996 = Peter R.Campbell, *Power and politics in Old Regime France 1720–1745*, Routledge, London, New York 1996..

Cieślak 1994 = Edmund Cieślak, *Stanisław Leszczyński*, Zakład Narodowy im. Ossolińskich, Wrocław-Warsaw-Cracow 1994.

39 Kuras 2018

Cosandey 2000 = Fanny Cosandey, *La reine de France: symbole et pouvoir, XVe-XVIIIe siècle*, Gallimard, Paris 2000.

Craveri 2007 = Benedetta Craveri, *Reines et favorites: le pouvoir des femmes*, Gallimard, Paris 2007.

Ferretti 2014 = Giulano Ferretti, "La politique italienne de la France et le duché de Savoie au temps de Richelieu", XVIIe siècle, 262 (1), 2014, 7–20.

Granovetter 1973 = Mark S. Granovetter, "The Strength of Weak Ties", American Journal of Sociology 78 (6), 1973, 1360–80.

Hartmann 1981 = Peter Claus Hartmann, "Zwei Wittelsbacher Prinzessinen am Hof Ludwigs XIV: Maria Anna Christina von Bayern und Elisabeth Charlotte von der Palatinate". Zeitschrift für Bayerische Landesgeschichte 44, 1981, 269–89.

Hatton 1969 = Ragnhild M. Hatton, *Charles XII of Sweden*, Weidenfeld and Nicholson, London 1969.

Hohkamp 2007 = Michaela Hohkamp. *Sisters, Aunts and Cousins : Familial Architectures and the Politcal Field in Early Modern Europe*, in: *Kinship in Europe: Approaches to Long-Term Developments (1300–1900)*, ed. Jon Mathieu, Simon Teuscher, David Sabean, Berghahn, New York 2007.

Hours 2006 = Bernard Hours, *La vertu et le secret. Le dauphin, fils de Louis XV*, Honoré Champion, Paris 2006.

Kohler 1994= Alfred Kohler, "Tu felix Austria nube…": Vom Klischee zur Neubewertung dynastischer Politik in der neueren Geschichte", Zeitschrift für historische Forschung 21, 1994, 461–482.

Kraus 1981 = Andreas Kraus, "Das Haus Wittelsbach und die europäischen Dynastien: Ergebnisse und Ausblick", Zeitschrift für Bayerische Landesgeschichte 44 (1), 1981, 425–452.

Kuras 2018 = Katarzyna Kuras, *Dwór królowej Marii Leszczyńskiej. Ludzie, pieniądze i wpływy*, Historia Iagellonica, Cracow 2018.

McGowan 2016 = *Dynastic Marriages 1612/1615. A Celebration of the Habsburg and Bourbon Unions*, ed. Margaret M. McGowan, Taylor & Francis, New York 2016.

Morton, Watanabe O'kelly 2016 = *Queens Consort, Cultural Transfer and European Politics, c.1500–1800*, ed. Adam Morton, Helen Watanabe-O'Kelly, Routledge, London-New York 2016.

Muratori-Philip 2010 = Anne Muratori-Philip, *Marie Leszczyńska : épouse de Louis XV*, Pygmalion, Paris 2010.

Neville, Skogh 2017 = *Queen Hedvig Eleonora and the Arts. Court Culture in Seventeenth Century Northern Europe*, ed. Kristoffer Neville, Lisa Skogh, Routledge, London, New York 2017.

Nicklas = Thomas Nicklas, „Unir de cœur et d'interest. La Bavière, la Savoie, la France et le choix des princesses au XVIIe siècle", XVIIe siècle 243 (2), 2009, 257–66.

Nolhac 1900 = Pierre de Nolhac, *Louis XV et Marie Leczinska : d'après de nouveaux documents*, Goupil, Paris 1900.

Porazinski 1999 = Jarosław Porazinski, *Epiphania Poloniae. Orientacje i postawy polityczne szlachty polskiej w dobie wielkiej wojny północnej (1702–1710)*, Wydawnictwo Uniwersytetu Mikołaja Kopernika, Toruń 1999.

Proyart 1825 = Liévin-Bonaventure Proyart, *Vie de Marie Leckzinska, princesse de Pologne, reine de France écrite sur les mémoires de la cour*, L. Lefort, Lille 1825.

Raynal 1887 = Paul Raynal, *Le mariage d'un roi 1721–1725*, Calmann Levy, Paris 1887.

Rogister 2004 = John Rogister, "Queen Marie Leszczyńska and faction at the French Court 1725–1768", in: Queenship in Europe 1660–1815, ed. Clarissa Campbell Orr, Cambridge University Press, Cambridge 2004, 186–216.

Rostworowski 1963 = Emanuel Rostworowski, *Jeszcze o ślubie Marii Leszczyńskiej i polskiej koronie*, in: *Legandy i fakty XVIII w.*, PWN, Warsaw 1963, 9–65.

Samsel 2007 = Agnieszka Samsel, "Dyplomacja i ceremoniał dworski wokół małżeństwa Ludwika XV z Marią Leszczyńską. Próba interpretacji", Scripta minora V, 267–325.

Schönpflug 2010 = Daniel Schönpflug, *Dynastic networks*, in: European History Online (EGO) EGO), published by the Institute of European History (IEG), Mainz 2010. http://www.ieg-ego.eu/schoenpflugd-2010-en, accessed 10.11.2020.

Smuts 2015 = Malcolm Smuts, *Religion, European Politics and Henrietta Maria's Circle, 1625–41*, in: *Henrietta Maria: Piety, Politics and Patronage*, ed. Erin Griffey, Taylor & Francis, New York 2015, 13–38.

Tischer 2008 = Anuschka Tischer, *Verwandtschaft als Faktor französischer Außenpolitik: Auswirkungen und Grenzen dynastischer Politik im 17. Jahrhundert*, in: *Grenzüberschreitende Familienbeziehungen: Akteure und Medien des Kulturtransfers in der Frühen Neuzeit*, hg. Dorothea Nolde, Claudia Opitz, Böhlau Verlag, Cologne-Weimar-Vienna 2008, 39–53.

Van Der Cruysse 2001 = Dirk Van der Cruysse, *Madame sein ist ein ellendes Handwerck. Liselotte von der Palatinate. Eine deutsche Prinzessin am Hof des Sonnenkönigs*, Piper, Munich 2001.

Wyleżyńska 1923 = Aurelia Wyleżyńska, *Marja Leszczyńska na dworze Wersalskim*, Wydawnictwo Polskie, Poznań-Lwów 1923.

Contributors

Aleksandra Barwicka-Makula, University of Silesia, Katowice
https://orcid.org/0000-0001-8053-5694
aleksandra.barwicka@us.edu.pl
PhD in humanities, historian, employed at the Institute of History at the University of Silesia in Katowice. A member of the Research Team on Royal Courts and Power Elites in the Tadeusz Manteuffel Institute of History at the Polish Academy of Sciences. The author of the book *Od wrogości do przyjaźni. Habsburgowie austriaccy wobec Polski w latach 1587–1592* (Katowice 2019), nominated to the Wacław Felczak and Henryk Wereszycki Award. At present, she continues tasks for the international project carried out by Professor Ryszard Skowron, the aim of which is to edit letters exchanged between the representatives of the Vasa and Habsburg dynasties ("The House of Vasa and The House of Austria. Correspondence from the Years 1587 to 1668"). In addition, she works on diplomatic contacts in the Polish-Lithuanian Commonwealth with the Habsburg states at the turn of the 16th and 17th century. She conducts research on foreign affairs and domestic policies of Sigismund III Vasa and the life at court in the times of the first Vasa ruler on the Polish throne. She is also interested in the lives of Polish queens who came from the Habsburg dynasty. She is passionate about Vincent van Gogh's paintings, the pre-war architecture of Silesia, old porcelain, and 1960s designs.

Agnieszka Januszek-Sieradzka, The John Paul II Catholic University of Lublin
https://orcid.org/0000-0002-3227-3797
agnieszka.januszek-sieradzka@kul.pl
Assistant Professor in humanities, historian, employed at the Institute of History at the John Paul II Catholic University of Lublin, co-ordinator of the Institute's didactics section, laureate of the University Chancellor's awards. A member and secretary of the Commission to the History of Bohemia and Polish-Czech Relations at the Polish Academy of Sciences, a member of the Research Team on Royal Courts and Power Elites at the Polish Academy of Sciences and the KUL Academic Society. She participates in research grants. She carries out research on the early modern history of Poland, particularly on the reign of the Jagiellonian dynasty, royal court and its culture, old-Polish epistolography, and the history of women, as well as the early modern history of the region and economy. She is the Author of several dozen articles and academic books: *Rezydencja królewska w Niepołomicach w czasach panowania króla Zygmunta Augusta, 1548–1572* (Lublin 2006) and *Królowa Barbara Radziwiłłówna w dworskim mikroświecie* (Lublin 2017). Editor and co-

editor of several monographs. Since 2009, she had been an editor of the series *Praeclara stirps Jagiellonica,* which publishes works on the Jagiellonian era written by young scholars. Organiser and co-organiser of several local and international academic conferences and a speaker at more than thirty symposia and conferences. She carries out popularisation activities aimed at a wide audience.

Katarzyna Kuras, The Jagiellonian University
https://orcid.org/0000-0002-6198-7131
katarzyna.kuras@uj.edu.pl
Assistant Professor in humanities, historian, specialising in the history of the 17th–18th century. She works on the history of the Polish-Lithuanian Commonwealth in the Saxon period, with a particular interest in client relations, patronage, and the significance of magnates' courts in the then political and cultural reality. She is the Author of the book *Współpracownicy i klienci Augusta A. Czartoryskiego w czasach saskich* (Historia Iagellonica, Cracow 2010). The second area of her interest is the 18th-century French court, particularly in the times of Louis XV. She is the Author of the book *Dwór królowej Marii Leszczyńskiej. Ludzie, pieniądze i wpływy* (Historia Iagellonica, Cracow 2018). At present, she works on cultural connections between the 18th century European courts, with a particular emphasis on the relations between Paris and Dresden in the times of Maria Josepha of Saxony, the daughter of Augustus III of Poland and the wife of Louis, Dauphin of France.

Damien Mallet, Bordeaux
damien_mallet@outlook.com
PhD in the Humanities, specialisation in history. He is a specialist in modern and contemporary history. He attended the Université Bordeaux Montaigne in France as well as Nicolaus Copernicus University in Toruń, Poland. He earned his doctorate with his joint-supervised thesis *Ce pays de Cocagne où les choses changent si souvent, le regard de Pierre des Noyers, secrétaire de la reine Louise-Marie, sur la Pologne de son temps (1645–1693),* under the supervision of Pr. Michel Figeac and Jarosław Dumanowski. In 2018, he received a research grant from the Centre de Recherche du Château de Versailles. His main themes of research are Pierre des Noyers, scholar and secretary of the Queen of Poland, Louise- Marie, Prince of Condé's bid for the Polish-Lithuanian throne, and French-Polish relations. He worked under the supervision of Chantal Grell on *Correspondance de Johannes Hevelius - Tome III. Correspondance avec Pierre des Noyers, secrétaire de la Reine de Pologne, 1646–1686* (Brepols 2020).

Anna Miączewska
PhD in the Humanities, specialisation in history; her written works include articles published in Polish and foreign academic journals; in 2015 her work on the

iconography of oil lamps was published by the Institute of European Culture at Adam Mickiewicz University in Poznań, Poland (*Roman Discus Lamps: Studies in the Significance and Meaning of Gladiatorial Images*, Gniezno 2015: Acta Humanistica Gnesnensia, vol. V). She is the co-editor of an academic monograph (*An Undiscovered Woman: from Antiquity to Modern Times*, (Lublin 2017: Maria Curie-Skłodowska University Press). She is currently working on the final version of her book about advertising in ancient Pompeii. She specialises in translating academic works (in the field of history and archaeology) into English.

Agnieszka Pawłowska-Kubik, Medical University of Gdańsk
https://orcid.org/0000-0002-7379-8645
agnieszkapawl@wp.pl
PhD in the Humanities, specialisation in history (2016), graduated Nicolaus Copernicus University in Toruń (Masters Degree in History and Polish Philology), currently works in the Department of History and Philosophy of Medical Sciences at Medical University of Gdańsk. Her research interests include the political history of the Polish-Lithuanian Commonwealth with particular interest in conflicts between the nobility and rulers, early modern medicine, health issues of the kings of the Polish-Lithuanian Commonwealth, and exenteration in the early modern times. She is a secretary of "Rocznik Gdański" editorial department, and a member of Gdańsk Academic Society and Association of Families of Soldiers of the Polish Underground State "Osuchy 1944". A scholarship holder of the Polish Historical Mission in Würzburg and the Lanckoroński Foundation, awarded in the competition "Complex and Simple" in 2015 under the patronage of the Ministry of Science and Higher Education. The author of several dozens of academic and popular science publications and materials for history teachers. Currently, she works on a book on Anna Jagiellon's letters.

Dominika Rychel-Mantur, University of Silesia, Katowice
https://orcid.org/0000-0001-8273-7417
dominika.mantur@us.edu.pl
PhD in humanities, historian, employed at the Institute of History at the University of Silesia in Katowice. She focuses her research on the elites of the Polish-Lithuanian Commonwealth and the period after the Partitions of Poland. She places particular emphasis on biographies and answers to research questions regarding the motivation and value system of individuals, and mechanisms of their careers, as well as their public activity. She is the Author of articles in academic journals, i.e. "Członkowie Rządu Centralnego Tymczasowego Wojskowego Galicji – przyczynek do biografii zbiorowej" (*UR Journal of Humanities and Social Sciences*, no. 3 (16)/ 2020, p. 23–38), and chapters in monographs, i.e. "Topografia miasta" (*Oświęcim – miasto pogranicza*, vol. 2, Warsaw 2018, p. 165–177). She was a speaker at con-

ferences on the elites of the Polish-Lithuanian Commonwealth, i.e. "Wielkie rody polsko-litewskie. „Wolni z wolnymi" – unia lubelska 1569–2019. Geneza, znaczenie, inspiracje w 450. rocznicę powstania unii polsko-litewskiej", Tarnobrzeg 2019. In 2018 she successfully defended her doctoral dissertation on a politician living at the turn of the 18th and 19th century: *Polityk dwóch epok. Tadeusza Matuszewicza (1765–1819) działalność publiczna*. This work will soon be published by the Silesian University Press.

Aleksandra Skzypietz, University of Silesia
https://orcid.org/0000-0003-1504-9950
aleksandra.skrzypietz@us.edu.pl
Associate Professor in humanities, historian, lecturer at the University of Silesia. A member of the Research Team on Royal Courts and Power Elites at the Polish Academy of Sciences; a participant of research grants. Her academic research includes: relations between Poland and France in the 17th and 18th century, organisation of the royal court in the modern period, the history and political significance of the Sobieski family, the influence of education on shaping political and civil attitudes, and the role of women in socio-political changes in the modern period. The Author of books: *Królewscy synowie – Jakub, Aleksander i Konstanty Sobiescy*, Katowice 2011; *Rozkwit i upadek rodu Sobieskich*, Warsaw 2014; *Jakub Sobieski*, Poznań 2015; *Królowa Margot. Ostatnia perła Walezjuszów*, Warsaw 2016; *Franciszek Ludwik de Bourbon, książę de Conti – "obrany król Polski". Saga rodu Kondeuszów*, Katowice 2019. At present, she is working on a biography of James Stuart's wife, Maria Clementina Sobieska.

Index of persons